hip-hop

redemption

Engaging Culture

WILLIAM A. DYRNESS
AND ROBERT K. JOHNSTON,
SERIES EDITORS

The Engaging Culture series is designed to help Christians respond with theological discernment to our contemporary culture. Each volume explores particular cultural expressions, seeking to discover God's presence in the world and to involve readers in sympathetic dialogue and active discipleship. These books encourage neither an uninformed rejection nor an uncritical embrace of culture, but active engagement informed by theological reflection.

hip-hop
redemption

finding god in the rhythm and the rhyme

Ralph Basui Watkins

Baker Academic

a division of Baker Publishing Group
Grand Rapids, Michigan

Published by Baker Academic
a division of Baker Publishing Group
P.O. Box 6287, Grand Rapids, MI 49516-6287
www.bakeracademic.com

Printed in the United States of America

Library of Congress Cataloging-in-Publication Data
Watkins, Ralph Basui, 1962–
    Hip-hop redemption : finding God in the rhythm and the rhyme / Ralph Basui Watkins.
        p. cm. — (Engaging culture)
    Includes bibliographical references and index.
    ISBN 978-0-8010-3311-7 (pbk.)
    1. Rap (Music)—Religious aspects—Christianity. 2. Hip-hop—Religious aspects—
Christianity. I. Title.
    ML3921.8R36W38 2011
    782.421649—dc22   2011016520

Scripture quotations are from the Holy Bible, New International Version® NIV®. Copyright © 1973, 1978, 1984, 2011 by Biblica, Inc.™ Used by permission of Zondervan. All rights reserved worldwide. www.zondervan.com.

11   12   13   14   15   16   17   7   6   5   4   3   2   1

This work is dedicated to the love of my life,
my wife Dr. Vanessa C. Watkins.

You have been my rhythm, my rhyme, and the reason I live.
I love you to life.

Thanks for always believing in me and encouraging me
to mix, remix, and write.

contents

introduction

The Mix and the Remix

As we begin our move into the culture of hip-hop, I ask that you walk with me and try, at least for a minute, to put your judgment in check as we go down this road. I ask for your patience, because it will allow you to hear what otherwise you might miss. Michael Dyson calls this suspending of judgment "ethical patience." To have ethical patience, the listener/reader attempts to empathize with the formidable array of choices, conflicts, and dilemmas that hip-hop is faced with. A person with ethical patience does not condemn hip-hop without first seeking to understand hip-hop and the hip-hop generation.[1] I invite you to ride with me as we take a journey in this book through the storied world of hip-hop. As you ride through the hip-hop story, you will see, hear, and feel the truth in the story. Toward the end of the text, I provide a set of lenses to help you make evaluative judgments of hip-hop culture that are linked to biblical principles.

The central question in this work is, how is hip-hop redemptive? In this question, I am not trying to redeem hip-hop. Rather, I want to argue that there is something inherently redeeming within hip-hop culture. To this end, I am claiming that there is a power in hip-hop and that it has theological resources.

Jon Michael Spencer said that all popular music is theological and coined the term *theomusicology* to denote his approach to interpreting musical traditions. Popular music is theological, Spencer says, because religion is "all-pervasive in culture." People are "inescapably" and naturally religious; we naturally ask and reflect on ultimate questions. Popular music reveals how people "ponder myriad vital questions that arise out of our sense of finiteness." Therefore, popular music provides a truer window into the human soul and reveals "a more honest religious discourse."[2] Spencer is suggesting that popular music is "truer" or more honest than what is commonly referred to as Christian or religious music. David Fillingim adds to the observation of Spencer when he says, "Popular music reflects the religious imagination unfettered by the chains of doctrinal propriety."[3] These are bold claims, but they have merit, and this text will tease out the merit of these claims.

James Cone, in his book *The Spirituals and the Blues*,[4] and David Fillingim, in his book *Redneck Liberation*, have both explored what Spencer suggests. This present book is yet another effort in that direction. I am seeking to find the redemptive power in hip-hop culture by making seven distinct moves in the following seven chapters. Each chapter title is influenced by a famous part of hip-hop culture. This cultural artifact is part name and part inspiration for the chapter and influences the direction of the chapter. These titles are important and should serve as key breaks as we mix it up.

The central question in this work is, how is hip-hop redemptive? In this question, I am not trying to redeem hip-hop. Rather, I want to argue that there is something inherently redeeming within hip-hop culture.

In chapter 1, "When Did You Fall in Love with Hip-hop? My Story and the Story of Hip-Hop," I share my struggle with hip-hop culture and the questions that birthed the project that led to this book. I start with my story because it is important to understand the writer so as to put his or her reflections in context. Chapter 2, "I Said a Hip-Hop: A Snapshot of Hip-Hop History," provides an introduction to hip-hop culture. It outlines a brief history of hip-hop, with reference to major works of and on hip-hop. The goal of this chapter is to introduce you to hip-hop while pointing you to the major hip-hop cultural and scholarly artifacts. You are encouraged to experience the artifacts mentioned in this chapter as well as those listed at the end of each chapter. Chapter 3, "R U Still Down? Hip-Hop Culture as an Extension of the Blues," contends that hip-hop culture and rap music didn't fall from the sky. Other ethnic groups have been a part of the hip-hop culture and adopted it, but hip-hop is still considered a child of the African American arts community. This chapter charts the history of African American music culture while making a direct link with the blues, rhythm and blues, and gospel, as these forms live on in hip-hop and rap.

Chapter 4, "I Used to Love Her and I Still Love Her: Loving the Broken Beauty of Hip-Hop," tries to help you move beyond the obvious. How do we develop a way to be a part of hip-hop and not feel dirty? How do we deal with our love for an art form and a culture that appear to be sexist, misogynist, and racy? How do we embrace the contradictions and deal with them in an engaging and constructive manner? What do we do with the sexism, violence, and misogyny in hip-hop? You will hopefully come out of this chapter understanding hip-hop as a subject and a culture that can be studied, loved, enjoyed, and critiqued. Chapter 5, "'Slippin' and Slidin' I'm about to Give Up': The Theological Truth in the Story," is the pivotal chapter in the book. This chapter does two things. First, it provides a case study of DMX, and second, it situates him and hip-hop in their proper sociohistorical context. The formula and power in hip-hop are found in the story. This chapter dissects this formula while empowering you with a method for unpacking these stories. The socio-theological method is applied as a tool of analysis in this chapter as the story of DMX is paralleled with the Joseph story of the Old Testament. I offer the model used in this chapter as a way to exegete hip-hop culture socio-theologically.

An encounter with a hip-hop theologian is the central task of chapter 6, "God Skipped Past the Church: A Hip-Hop Theology and a Hip-Hop Theologian." Talib Kweli's album *Eardrum* is used as the text for exegeting a hip-hop theological perspective as I share the overt theological reflections of one of hip-hop's leading socio-theologians. As the book comes to a close, the final chapter, "*The Miseducation of Lauryn Hill*: A Socio-Theological Critique of Hip-Hop," builds on the two previous chapters by looking directly at the theological moves and redemptive nature of hip-hop while critiquing hip-hop from a biblical perspective. This critique is cast in light of the women who have been a part of hip-hop culture. Their work and voices are employed as we deal directly with the oppressive nature of hip-hop culture that can't be excused. The misogyny, sexism, and violence in hip-hop must be dealt with head-on. This final chapter calls us both to appreciate and to critique hip-hop culture from a biblical perspective while providing a frame for that critical appreciation. In the conclusion, I go back to chapter 1 and connect the loose ends with this extended remix.

The conversation that starts in this book continues online. I blog weekly at www.hiphopredemption.org, providing support for pastors, churches, professors, and students as they seek to engage the theology embedded in hip-hop culture. The website also features companion material—including discussion questions—for this book. You can also join the conversation on my Facebook page "hip-hop redemption" and check out my videos on Vimeo at www.vimeo.com/channels/218503.

Publishers Note: Please be advised that this book attempts an honest and critical engagement with artistic material some readers may find offensive.

when did you fall in love with hip-hop?

My Story and the Story of Hip-Hop

So, when did you fall in love with hip-hop?

Sidney Shaw, *Brown Sugar*

For God so loved the world that he gave his one and only Son, that whoever believes in him shall not perish but have eternal life. For God did not send his Son into the world to condemn the world, but to save the world through him.

John 3:16–17

An Extended Track

The movie *Brown Sugar* opens with Sanaa Lathan's character, Sidney Shaw, a journalist, asking the question, "So, when did you fall in love with hip-hop?" Then a series of famous hip-hop personalities answer the question. I fell in love with this movie, and the opening of the movie provides a model to open this book. The opening is a series of jump cuts from one scene to the next. Hip-hop is like jump cuts, abrupt starts and stops, that are woven into a tapestry we call hip-hop culture. Hip-hop is a mixture of the old that has been made new in the remix. I begin this book with a series of jump cuts as I share how my life and hip-hop intersect while speaking of the revelations and transformations that came along the way. Yes, I love hip-hop, and this has been a love affair. I believe my job—much like that of Jesus—isn't to condemn hip-hop or condemn the world. Jesus came in love and with love. This is a love story. My love story with hip-hop goes like this.

As much as I love hip-hop, I will always come to hip-hop as an outsider. I am an African American in his mid-forties. I was raised on rhythm and blues with a touch of jazz. I am a child of that lonely AM radio station at the end of the dial that played the music of my people and went off the air at 6:00 p.m.

Hip-hop is like jump cuts, abrupt starts and stops, that are woven into a tapestry we call hip-hop culture. Hip-hop is a mixture of the old that has been made new in the remix.

When hip-hop emerged, my musical taste and cultural worldview were already formed. I start with this confession or positioning of myself because, as you read, I ask you to listen with who I am in mind. This book would sound different if I were thirty years old and thoroughly hip-hop. I accept the fact that I am a member of the "bridge generation"—the ones who birthed hip-hop as adults but soon thereafter handed it off to the next generation, which was bred, born, and raised thoroughly hip-hop. Bakari Kitwana describes the bridge generation: "Those folks, who were right at the cusp, were too young to be defined by civil rights/Black power and too old to be deemed hip-hop generationers. Nonetheless, they have played a pivotal role in this generation's development by linking both."[1]

As much as my generation has something to say about hip-hop as we engage the culture and the life, you should also be encouraged to engage children of the hip-hop nation. These are people like my daughters, who were raised on hip-hop and embrace the culture in a deep way that I will never be able to reach. I readily respect and admire their oneness with hip-hop. The things I share in this book are yet another remix (putting things together again) of my life with hip-hop as I live it with those who are hip-hop. Therefore, I start with myself and my story, because the voice of the storyteller as situated in history is as important as the story.

I was raised during the last throes of the civil rights movement. I was one of those children of the dream—one of those who were to inherit the blessings from the struggle of our elders.[2] The first evidence of the progress our elders had fought for appeared when I began the third grade in 1971. A small band of kids and I were transferred from Hungerford Elementary School in Eatonville, Florida, to Lake Sybellia Elementary School in Maitland, Florida. We were bused, but bused with an attitude (BWA). We were to become what Todd Boyd would later call the New Black Aesthetic, or the NBA generation. We were going to Lake Sybellia to get access to the power that had been denied our parents. Boyd says, "The NBA have grown up in the post–civil rights era and see individual power and access to the means of representation as significant goals."[3] We epitomized what Boyd describes in his work: we went to that white school with the mission to get power and education and use them as a means to represent blackness on our terms. My mother and her friends drilled into my head that I was to go to that school to get all they had to offer. I was to be a success for my people. I worked hard while priding myself on being a pint-size revolutionary. So there I was—a bright child, one of the few black kids in that school, all the time listening to soul music with a revolutionary zeal fed, supported, and developed by my elders.

Gil Scott-Heron: the one who introduced me to rap

This era was also characterized by the infusion of disco music. My generation saw a move from rhythm and blues to music that, with an infusion of disco, would morph into rap. In my teen years, my brother, Victor Watkins, turned me on to conscious music. Conscious music was politically motivated, socially aware, and raised issues relevant to the continuing struggles of poor and brown people. My friends and I listened to Gil Scott-Heron and Brian Jackson. The song "Rapper's Delight" didn't introduce me to rap music; Gil Scott-Heron introduced me to rap. I can't give you an exact date when I first heard him rap over beats or recite his poems in time. I do remember that my commitment to the liberation struggle of African Americans was linked to the early rap I heard on records and from my mother's friends. "Mother" Earlene Watkins, a community organizer/political activist, raised me, and she frequently held meetings of her friends at our house. I was the little revolutionary, like Michael on the show *Good Times*. I idolized Malcolm X early on; Martin Luther King Jr. became a hero of mine later in life. Scott-Heron helped me hear and posit my thinking in real time with real issues. It had to be around the late-1970s that I heard "The Revolution Will Not

Be Televised" by Scott-Heron. That was the beginning of my love affair with rap music and what would later be labeled hip-hop by DJ Hollywood.[4]

I continued to listen to Scott-Heron and Brian Jackson, but as hip-hop grew, so did my attention to hip-hop culture. Scott-Heron and the Last Poets were rap to me. But then the Sugarhill Gang's "Rapper's Delight" saw the light of day in 1979, and that year marked a move for me and hip-hop culture as we found a new life together. Hip-hop was moving away from the conscious to the playful. The Sugarhill Gang was birthed in 1979 by Sylvia Robinson of Sugar Hill Records. They weren't like the Last Poets or Gil Scott-Heron and Brian Jackson. (Interesting that Robinson chose to call them a gang.) The early groups grew up together, performed together as a part of living in the community. This move from an organic aesthetic, in which groups developed communally, to a new wave or new type of rap artist began with Sugar Hill Records and the Sugarhill Gang.

The American roots of this hip-hop culture were in the South Bronx party culture. DJ Kool Herc, Grandmaster Flash, and their disciples were more concerned with having fun than they were with stimulating political revolution or thought. Interestingly, this shift occurred on the eve of the Reagan administration inauguration, and the sociocontextualization of the growth of hip-hop is central to this study. It was during the Regan era that civil rights would go into retrenchment, inner cities would fall into decay, and the trickle-down theory of economics would prevail but never trickle to the 'hood. As Regan took the throne, hip-hop stood up to cry out from the city.

During the eight years from 1980 to 1988, hip-hop culture came of age, with many twists and turns. The recording and release of Kurtis Blow's "The Breaks," from his album *Kurtis Blow*, marked a break (pun intended) from the party/dance music that was emerging from hip-hop culture. "The Message" by Grandmaster Flash and the Furious Five was another blip on the screen, as it, like "The Breaks," was a conscious rap song. "The Message," ironically, was a song the group didn't want to record, and it was a song they didn't write. Sylvia Robinson acquired the song and presented it to Grandmaster Flash and the Furious Five, who thought it wasn't a party-type song and felt it would hurt their relationship with their party audience. In the end, however, they recorded the song, and it was well received by the hip-hop nation.

As much as early rap was party rap, when you explore the narratives of early rap, you can hear the story of struggle from inner-city streets. This evolution and history of hip-hop are central to this work: if we are to understand and appreciate hip-hop culture, we must get a sense of both the larger sociocultural history that surrounds hip-hop and the specific circumstances in which hip-hop culture developed. In other words, we must be conscious of the context out of which hip-hop evolved. The biography of hip-hop is bolstered by the stories of the artists, which help us hear the truth, redemption, theology, and liberation that is in hip-hop. Our quest is for the redemptive and theological implications embedded in hip-hop culture.

In many ways, my relationship with hip-hop follows the ebb and flow of the culture. I moved away from the more party hip-hop and gravitated toward the more conscious rap music. Party hip-hop was only marginally related to my life in the early 1980s, because I was trying hard to be a good African Methodist Episcopal Church preacher, and my wife and I were raising young children. I was lost in church and out of touch with the larger world for the most part. In the late 1980s, I took off for seminary and found hip-hop again. I went to seminary in Dubuque, Iowa, not far from Chicago, Illinois. Many of the African American students came to Dubuque from the inner city of Chicago. As director of minority student affairs and a hall director of a male residence hall for the University of Dubuque, I was in contact with undergraduates daily. They listened to hip-hop and watched Black Entertainment Television (BET), and I established a connection with them through hip-hop. I found myself in hip-hop and hip-hop in me as I returned to it in the late 1980s.

[The] evolution and history of hip-hop are central to this work: if we are to understand and appreciate hip-hop culture, we must get a sense of both the larger sociocultural history that surrounds hip-hop and the specific circumstances in which hip-hop culture developed.

The most memorable albums for me during this time were Boogie Down Productions' *Criminal Minded* and *Ghetto Music: The Blueprint of Hip-Hop* and Public Enemy's two classic albums, *It Takes a Nation of Millions to Hold Us Back* and *Fear of a Black Planet*. These four albums were *good* hip-hop. Listen to my value judgment here. These albums were revolutionary. These albums weren't held hostage by the party culture, overt sexism, or misogyny that were beginning to dominate hip-hop. I could listen with black intellectual and Christian pride. I thought I could discard the other hip-hop. Some would say I was a hip-hop schizophrenic, while others would say I was just being a wise Christian. After all, I was growing in my faith, was a seminary student, and was becoming much more selective about what I listened to.

I continued to listen to hip-hop, justifying it as a way of getting to know my students. The truth is, I enjoyed the music, though I didn't care a whole lot for some of the videos. I enjoyed the fun in hip-hop. I liked the songs that made you move, the songs you just couldn't fight, the songs that made you nod your head. Even when you tried not to move, they would make you move. Over time, my listening extended to include the breadth and depth of hip-hop. Though I was still caught in the dilemma of how ethical it was to enjoy songs like "Baby Got Back" or "Wild Thang" or "Funky Cold Medina" or "I Need Love," I must confess I enjoyed them. I was drawn to the beauty of hip-hop culture. At times I was haunted by the questions, what am I doing? and what should I be doing?

but I was not alone. Saul Williams, a poet, musician, child of hip-hop, and son of a Pentecostal minister, described his struggles listening to hip-hop in the mid-1990s as well: "I couldn't listen to hip-hop the same way. I felt personally attacked whenever an emcee was misusing his power. I grew angry at the way capitalism and violence was being romanticized."[5] I shared Williams's sentiments, but I continued to listen and watch. I was judging hip-hop while enjoying hip-hop. As my daughters and my son were growing up, I wondered what they were getting from the music as they watched music videos with their babysitter, who always arrived with headphones on and immediately turned the television to BET.

Track 1: Confronted by Tupac

When I left seminary and went to work at Clarion University in Clarion, Pennsylvania, as director of minority student affairs, I was hit smack in the face with hip-hop again. I was now dealing with hardcore East Coast rap in all its manifestations. Once again I had to listen in to communicate effectively with college students.

From Clarion University I went to inner-city Pittsburgh to pastor Trinity African Methodist Episcopal Church and evangelize working-class African Americans. The young men and women of the Hill District of Pittsburgh pushed me to listen to hip-hop. Tone, a young teenager from the Hill District, said, "Yo, Rev. If you want to know wassup, you got to get to Tupac." I confronted Tone and his friends about their embrace of Tupac and other rappers of the day, but in the end they convinced me to listen with them and to interact with hip-hop in my sermons and Bible studies. I learned from them not only that Tupac had something to say to them but also that Tupac and hip-hop had something to say to me and the church. I resonated with the edginess and hardness of hip-hop. I began to rap or freestyle from the pulpit. The crowd would go wild when I would break out in rhyme. During those moments in the pulpit, I began to feel a positive spiritual power in hip-hop, as if God was in hip-hop.

As a young pastor, I was out of the loop, but hip-hop put me back in the loop and in touch with the culture of the working-class African American community I was trying to serve. I wasn't the normal pastor in our denomination. We did street witnessing and club evangelism. We even took the pews out of the church and put them in the streets to preach the gospel. Yes, this was me and is me. I will never forget the major turning point in my life as it relates to the power of hip-hop and my ministry. This major turning point was the seed that produced what we are now listening to, writing, and rewriting together. Remember that this book is a remix. As you read, you are cutting and scratching on the ones and twos (turntables). As you process and reconfigure, outline, highlight, and write your notes in the margin, they blend with the mix that I, along with the Holy Spirit, have produced in this book. Hip-hop is never a completed work; it is always a work calling to be remixed. Please do your remix.

The major turning point for me and hip-hop as it relates to my ministry took place in 1996. To be exact, it was the week of September 9, 1996. It was one of the longest weeks in hip-hop history. Tupac was shot four times in Las Vegas and was admitted to the hospital. As the week progressed, the reports indicated that our never-say-die brother was on the ropes. On Wednesday night, the youth turned out as always for the weekly Bible study. The church was packed, and the topic on the minds of the young brothers and sisters was Tupac. By this time I had embraced Tupac and hip-hop. I lifted up a prayer for Tupac and his family. At the end of the night, a few of the young brothers hung around to talk to me. One was Tone, who had no address and no real home but was hungry for love. Tone and his peers loved Tupac, and their love was expressed that night in the form of anticipatory grief.

On Friday evening, September 13, 1996, Tupac died. I, like so many, couldn't believe he was dead. I watched the television news story over and over in disbelief. Tupac was our hero; he was the one who had been shot and had appeared in court the next day. He was no mere mortal; he had already come back from the dead. As I moved to accept the fact that Tupac was dead, I immediately began to rework my sermon for Sunday. I knew that this week I had to preach to the balcony—the place where most of my teenagers sat. I also knew that many of the people who sat on the floor were peers of Tupac as well.

That Sunday I went to church early and prayed. As the service began, I noticed that many of the young brothers who were the biggest Tupac followers weren't there. When the church van returned from the second run, the driver reported that they hadn't been waiting at the stop. I immediately told my assistant minister to keep the service going until I got back. I got in my van and found those brothers. They came with me with no resistance. They were broken and in mourning. I had to have a word that day, but the word didn't come from me; it came from God through Tupac. This was the revelatory moment I needed.

Tupac had something to say. I took Tupac's catalog of recordings and his life story and put them in dialogue with the Bible, and in the end we heard God through hip-hop. The theological questions Tupac was raising were making me rethink my theology. It was Tupac who put flesh and bones on the theology that was to inform my preaching. Something I thought was impossible a few years before had happened. God had moved me from being a skeptic and a critic to a person who could see and hear God in the music and message of hip-hop. As my drummer rapped out a beat, I began to freestyle. There I was, a seminary-trained preacher talking in rhyme, ministering via the power of hip-hop and the Holy Spirit in hip-hop. The Spirit of God was in hip-hop. Tone and others had opened me up to hear and listen to God in hip-hop, and now by the life and death of Tupac, I was born again with them as we became hip-hop together on that day. On Sunday, September 15, 1996, I was converted a second time as I came back home to hip-hop under full submission to God as a missionary to hip-hop and from hip-hop! Yes, I had fallen back in love with hip-hop.

Track 2: Nod Your Head: Good Morning, Hip-Hop, "I Feel You"

Is God in hip-hop? Is God omnipresent? These two questions push me as I reflect on hip-hop, and I want them to push you as you read this book. Is God in hip-hop? If I believe that God is omnipresent, which I do, then I must ask not if, but *how* God is in hip-hop. I will offer my reflections on how I have come to see God and hip-hop, and I invite you to reflect with me. I want to take you back to another experience I had in hip-hop that made me take these two questions more seriously than ever. On August 9, 2006, I was at the House of Blues in Anaheim, California. The featured performer was KRS-One, one of my all-time favorite emcees. KRS-One sounds more like a preacher than a rapper, or maybe rappers are preachers. Are rappers preachers? Are they walking and teaching by the power of the Holy Spirit? Tupac Shakur's mother, Afeni Shakur, said, "Artists are messengers from God. They get here on earth and express themselves because of Him."[6] Are these messengers, emcees, rappers from God? Is God in hip-hop? These questions cannot be dismissed; they demand serious reflection. As a matter of fact, this question is at the heart of this book.

> *If I believe that God is omnipresent, which I do, then I must ask not if, but* how *God is in hip-hop.*

Back to August 9: KRS-One led us into the spiritual force of hip-hop. I was taken in. I felt the music. The rhymes and freestyling moved me. The music went through me. I went to inspect the event as a detached socio-theological observer, but something happened. I was caught up in the moment, and I was moved. I was bobbing my head, tapping my feet. My mind was moving a mile a minute, my heart was thumping, and my spirit was being stirred. What was happening to me? Was this the Holy Spirit, or was it simply the rhythm of the music? Was this the cry of ancient Africa? What was happening? I didn't know it, but this is where my story begins a third time. I was finishing up a book for Judson Press at the time and doing research for the book you are reading. I didn't know where I was, in between books, and I was searching for how to put into words what I was struggling to write about. I was still trying to understand what happens in hip-hop as it relates to the Holy Spirit. What are the spiritual forces behind the music? What is it about hip-hop that I and so many resonate with? Is there redeeming, life-affirming power in hip-hop?

KRS-One: the teacher-entertainer

At this particular concert, KRS-One called on the Spirit as he took us to places I hadn't planned on going. He said, "I feel the Spirit in here tonight." At one point, he went to the sign behind him onstage that read "The House of Blues," and he remarked that it should be "The House of Hip-Hop." But then he confessed that there would be no hip-hop if there were no blues. KRS-One traced the history of hip-hop from the blues, through Jamaica via DJ Kool Herc, and then to North America, where the next evolution of African American culture was born. According to KRS-One, God created hip-hop. God spoke through the hands of the mothers and fathers of hip-hop. God touched DJ Kool Herc, and he heard the power in the breakdown portion of songs. The breakdown portion of the song is that part of the song, normally in the middle, where the beat is rich and deep, the music flows, and the dancers are at the peak of their engagement with the track. DJ Kool Herc was led to find a way to extend those break beats by looping them. Then along came Grandmaster Flash, the creative technical genius of hip-hop who fathered the spirit in Grand Wizard Theodore, and the masters of turntablism were born. In the late 1970s, the mother of popular hip-hop, Sylvia Robinson, gave life to the Sugarhill Gang, and the song "Rapper's Delight" was born through her and her record company in November 1979.

For hip-hop, the force behind the culture is something that can't be seen or touched. There is a spiritual force in hip-hop. What is this spiritual force? Is it redeeming, or is it destructive? These questions kept ringing in my head. Was my Tupac moment ten years earlier an isolated incident, or was God doing something in me through hip-hop again?

At the core of hip-hop are four basic principles. We chanted them over and over at the KRS-One concert that night: Peace! Love! Unity! Having fun![7] Are these four centerpieces of hip-hop still alive? Did the centerpieces of hip-hop get lost? Has hip-hop gone astray? If you listen to KRS-One, you might think that hip-hop has gone astray because KRS-One critiques popular hip-hop that we hear on the radio. There are camps in hip-hop. One camp is made up of the essentialists or purists like KRS-One, who contends that much of what masquerades as hip-hop doesn't embrace the four basic principles of hip-hop. As much as I am tempted to agree with KRS-One and the essentialists, I can't write off what hip-hop has become.

Hip-hop has evolved into a complex culture. One must take a deep look at the various strands of hip-hop and allow it to grow and not be held hostage by a 1980s developmental lens of "authenticity." One can critique the hip-hop industry while also accepting the core hip-hop culture, and maybe we can separate the two—the industry and the culture. To separate the core of the culture from the hip-hop industry might be like a wheat and chaff issue (Matt. 13:24–30), but maybe there is hope in looking at the two separately. Maybe there is a difference between what major record companies are selling in the consumer market and what remains at the core of hip-hop culture. There may also be embedded, even in the grossest commodification of hip-hop, the core values of peace, love, unity, and having fun.

These are questions we will have to work through together as we dialogue throughout this remix. Yes, I am leaving you hanging here. I am not clear what happened at that concert, but it produced the questions that became labor pains for this work.

Track 3: Interlude: Moving In and Out

As we attempt to navigate the murky waters of hip-hop throughout this text, I will point to the influence of the hip-hop industry while being conscious of the camps in hip-hop. Yet I will not fully delineate between what the essentialists call "real hip-hop" and what is now more popularly known as hip-hop culture or rap music. Hip-hop culture is built on the foundation of the music and the culture that preceded it. In the music, I will try to locate a theology. It is my contention that there is a theological core in hip-hop, and this is a theology of redemption as the beats and lyrics come together to give form and shape to a worldview. KRS-One talked about redemption and God throughout his concert, a concert that moved me and made me think deeper and more theologically about hip-hop than I ever had before. Theodor Adorno has pointed to a theological aspect of music, one I think was present in the experience I had at the KRS-One concert:

In comparison to signifying language, music is a language of a completely different type. Therein lies music's theological aspect. What music says is a proposition at once distinct and concealed. Its idea is the form [*Gestalt*] of the name of God. It is demythologized prayer, freed from the magic of making anything happen, the human attempt, futile, as always, to name the name itself, not to communicate meaning.[8]

Adorno points us in the right direction as we seek to understand the theological characteristics of hip-hop. The music or beats of hip-hop are blended with the rhymes of emcees and later interpreted by the people who are followers and participants in the creation of hip-hop. As the DJ, artist, and audience come together to understand, they each leave the room not quite having understood. The proposition of the music and the culture is still somewhat concealed. The demythologized prayer is not yet deciphered. They listen again and again, perform the piece publicly, listen in different venues, and they hear differently each time. They feel differently each time. The Spirit is working in the music in a new way. As God manifests Godself in this space, a holy encounter is enacted. Something mystical is happening, and the DJ, the artist, and the audience can't quite name what god this is—or what God is doing in hip-hop—but something is happening when the beat, the lyrics, the emcee, and the hip-hop nation meet for worship. God is present because God is omnipresent. God knows what is going on because God is omniscient. The culture communicates and makes meaning. It gives significance to lives and recognizes the unique struggles of the hip-hop generation. I know because I have been there with them. I've felt God, seen God, and recognized God move in the presence of hip-hop, even as God remained concealed.

It is my contention that there is a theological core in hip-hop, and this is a theology of redemption as the beats and lyrics come together to give form and shape to a worldview.

KRS-One took us on a spiritual journey that night. Something happened in that room. I can't quite name it. The beats moved us. The beats were laced with the rhymes, and there was an interaction among music, rhymes, and Spirit. We were all Rhymen (a form of Amen) to the music. As KRS-One took us down hip-hop memory lane, the rhymes from the past evoked a spiritual response. When KRS-One came off the stage and into the crowd, the spiritual energy level soared. A cipher (a circle of people who surround the performer) was formed, b-boys (break-boys, a.k.a. break dancers) went to the floor, and the crowd broke into an ecstatic state. The beats continued to pound in our spirits as we waved our hands in the air and bounced to the music. Up and down we bounced as the Spirit gave utterance. We were one nation that night: young and old, black, brown, red, yellow, white—all a part of the hip-hop nation. We went to church that night. As I walked back to my car, I felt as if I had just left a revival service. Was God there that night? Is God in hip-hop? Is there any good in hip-hop? Can God use hip-hop for his plan of redemption? Is hip-hop redemptive in its present form, which is presented in mainstream popular culture? More questions confront us as we take hip-hop seriously.

Over the next few chapters, I invite you to take a journey with me as we explore hip-hop. As you read, I implore you also to listen, watch, and become hip-hop. To become hip-hop means you enter the culture at a place where you find a connection or oneness with the culture. For me to become hip-hop, I became a DJ. For you it may mean being a more devoted and close listener to the culture via rap music. At the end of each chapter, I provide a guide to hip-hop: albums to listen to, movies to view, websites to visit. I encourage you to go to iTunes or the music source of your choice and purchase the items referenced. Or borrow a CD or DVD from a friend. It is important that you make a way to hear, feel, see, and touch. You touch hip-hop as you hold the album, CD, or other cultural artifact in your hands; you touch hip-hop by allowing it to change you. It is akin to an incarnational relationship with the culture that you are reading about. If you already have the music, listen again. You may find that at this point in your life you hear and feel the music differently. If this is your first time taking hip-hop seriously, I ask you to suspend any prejudice you may have and be open. Be open to experiencing hip-hop afresh. Watch videos of the music and engage the culture from all corners. Wear hip-hop clothing, walk hip-hop, talk hip-hop, live and feel hip-hop as you read this book. Hip-hop is a culture, and many hip-hoppas define themselves as hip-hop. Therefore, I implore you to get as close to being hip-hop as you can as you engage the culture and hip-hop—live and in color.

I am almost apologetic for writing a book about hip-hop, for hip-hop is not something we can read about and truly learn about if we are not willing to experience it. It is like writing about a powerful worship experience: the best of writers can't do it justice. In the words of my momma, "You had to be in church today." I am asking you to come to the hip-hop church with me as you encounter the spirit of hip-hop. There is something in hip-hop that begs not to be ignored. Saul Williams put it best when he said:

> There is no music more powerful than hip-hop. No other music so purely demands an instant affirmative on such a global scale. When the beat drops, people nod their heads, "yes," in the same way they would in conversation with a loved one, a parent, professor, or minister. Instantaneously, the same mechanical gesture that occurs in moments of dialogue as a sign of agreement which, subsequently, releases increased oxygen to the brain and, thus, broadens one's ability to understand, becomes the symbolic gesture that connects you to the beat. No other musical form has created such a raw and visceral connection to the heart while still incorporating various measures from other musical forms that then appeal to other aspects of the emotional core of an individual.[9]

Nod your head, as Will Smith says.[10] Hip-hop demands a response. You have to nod your head! As you read, I want you to bounce to the beat. This is the remix. I am bouncing to the beat of hip-hop as I strike the keys on my keyboard. Hip-hop is playing and leading me through the development of this text. Come on and bounce with me. This book is written in the spirit of hip-hop. It is about sampling and putting together a remix. I put the pieces of the culture together to form each cut (chapter), and now we have a complete album, which is called a book.

We are making music as we give this offering back to the culture. Adorno puts it this way: "To interpret music means to make music. Musical interpretation is the act of execution that holds fast to similarity to language, as synthesis, while at the same time it erases every individual incidence of that similarity. Hence, the idea of interpretation belongs to music essentially and is not incidental to it."[11] This book is music. It is written as an act of interpretation of the music that is at the foundation of a culture. This book is not to be read as much as it is to be listened to. It doesn't call for agreement, but it wants you to nod your head as you read. Feel the beat. To feel the beat doesn't mean that you agree with all that you hear. It means you feel what you are reading. If you can't feel hip-hop, you will never get close to understanding the spiritual power of hip-hop. Hip-hop is about a feeling and a filling. Hip-hop happens inside us. Hip-hop lives inside me!

Getting in Touch with Hip-Hop

Albums

I am a big proponent of definitive albums in hip-hop that define and represent the flavor of a period. I have listed the following in order of importance.

Run-D.M.C. *Run-D.M.C.* Profile/Arista, 1984. This album was a collection of their hits to date. It is essential hip-hop because Run-D.M.C., along with Jam Master Jay, was the first major crossover success in hip-hop.

Blow, Kurtis. *Christmas Rappin'*. Mercury, 1979; and *Kurtis Blow*. Mercury, 1980. These are next in the lineup of defining hip-hop.

Grandmaster Flash and the Furious Five. *The Adventures of Grandmaster Flash on the Wheels of Steel*. Sugar Hill, 1981. I recommended Run-D.M.C. and Kurtis Blow first because they were authentically born out of hip-hop culture. We have to remember that the Sugarhill Gang was put together by Sylvia Robinson and at least one of the members wasn't even a rapper. Sugar Hill Records has also reissued a five-disc set on Rhino Records titled *The Sugar Hill Records Story*, which is also worth listening to.

Boogie Down Productions. *Criminal Minded*. B-Boy, 1987; and *Ghetto Music: The Blueprint of Hip-Hop*. Jive, 1989.

Public Enemy. *It Takes a Nation of Millions to Hold Us Back*. Def Jam, 1988; and *Fear of a Black Planet*. Def Jam, 1990.

Films

Again, the following list is in order of importance.

Wild Style. Directed by Charlie Ahearn. Wild Style Productions, 1983. This is the first and a must.

Style Wars. Directed by Tony Silver and Henry Chalfant. Public Art Films, 1983. The power of graffiti cannot be lost or minimized in the cultural development of hip-hop culture. Graffiti style and flavor have fed the style we see in hip-hop now: colorful, big, and oversized. Graffiti provides an aesthetic in hip-hop that we see in clothes and tattoos.

Beat Street. Directed by Stan Lathan. Orion Pictures, 1984. This movie really captures snapshots of the early culture with cameos by figures like DJ Kool Herc.

Krush Groove. Directed by Michael Schultz. Warner Bros. Pictures, 1985. This is a classic grimy tale of the emerging hip-hop culture. The simple fact that Run-D.M.C. and the Fat Boys are in this movie makes it worth watching.

Scratch. Directed by Doug Pray. Firewalk Films, 2001. A trip into the world of the DJ is essential. I will argue later that the DJ/producer is the heart of hip-hop culture, with rap being the bloodline.

Brown Sugar. Directed by Rick Famuyiwa. Fox Searchlight, 2002.

Website

Davey D's Hip-Hop Corner: The New Source for the Hip-Hop Generation. www.daveyd.com.

i said a hip-hop

A Snapshot of Hip-Hop History

This Is Too Much for One CD

Rapper's Delight was the first major-selling hip-hop record. This classic record introduced the world to what would become known as hip-hop culture. They announced it on the anthem: "I said a hip-hop da hippy to the hippy to the hip-hop, ah you don't stop, rock it to the bang bang buggy, up jump the buggy to the rhythm of the bookdy beat." But before you hear that famous intro, it's the beat from Chic's "Good Times" that gets you. This wonderful marriage of a powerful beat via disco and rap lyrics birthed the baby that would grow up to be hip-hop. The beat, the DJ, and the rapper (emcee) would lead the way in embodying hip-hop culture. We say "hip-hop culture" because even though the emcees were rapping a song over the beat supplied by the DJ (or in this initial birth, a band), the flavor of the culture was wrapped up in the art form that was conveyed through the story. The way the rappers moved and dressed, the bravado and swagger that permeated their act, were hip-hop culture in its full embodiment. They were hip-hop as they told life stories in the form of a rap. This classic anthem starts by giving a shout out and a name to the culture.

The term *hip-hop* originated with DJ Hollywood, who would shout out the term while playing records.[1] Fab 5 Freddy, one of the early leaders of hip-hop culture, has suggested in his definition that those who attended a party the night before might describe the event as hip-hop, meaning the event was hip and it was hopping or full of energy. So from the beginning, hip-hop was about energy and being "all the way live." In the 1990s, when Lil John introduced us to crunk—music with heavy bass partnered with rock sensibilities that made people dance until they broke out in a sweat—he was actually returning hip-hop to its roots. Party or good-times music is the root of hip-hop culture.

Several well-written books provide a thorough history of hip-hop culture. The difficulty with books about hip-hop is that it is impossible to incorporate in any one book the breadth and depth of hip-hop culture. Invariably, authors tend to lean toward privileging a part of the culture. In the final analysis, books can't do hip-hop culture justice. Russell Potter said it best:

> The contents of this volume—or any other—do not and cannot represent the full range of hip-hop culture; at best they are snapshots of a movement. That is not to say that some snapshots aren't more useful than others—they are—but only that, until books become as fully multi-media as the culture(s) they discuss, they are always going to be substantially incomplete.[2]

This book, and especially this chapter, is just another snapshot. This book, like many others, leans on rap music and rap lyrics and emcees to tell the story.

One book that does a good job of being as inclusive and as balanced as possible is Jeff Chang's *Can't Stop, Won't Stop: A History of the Hip-Hop Generation*.[3] Chang includes the various strands of the culture in a unique way. He doesn't limit his analysis to rap music, but works to weave a rich cultural tapestry that includes graffiti, dance, emcees, and DJs. Chang's second book, *Total Chaos: The Art and Aesthetics of Hip-Hop* (an edited volume), continues his historical work while pointing readers to the future of hip-hop. These two books should be read in tandem. In the book *The Hip-Hop Years: A History of Rap*, Alex Ogg and David Upshal do an admirable job of introducing the popular rap records that laid the foundation for rap music,[4] and David Toop, in his *Rap Attack* books, adds to this history.[5] I mention these books and will refer to other cultural artifacts throughout this chapter so that you can utilize the sources that you feel will complete your remix. This chapter provides a brief survey of historical hip-hop moments, and you are encouraged to listen to, view, and read the cultural artifacts mentioned throughout this chapter.

I like to talk about hip-hop culture. I talk about hip-hop culture because it is difficult, if not impossible, to disentangle the intertwined history that is hip-hop culture. When we try to focus on graffiti, break dancing, DJing, or emceeing as separate historical trajectories, we run into problems. They are all tied together; they influence one another, touch one another, and are a part of one another. The best one can do is try to follow the various trajectories as a remixed collaboration,

Invariably, when one tries to listen to a freestyle, there is a line that isn't quite understood and can never be repeated in the way it was originally delivered. This is hip-hop: it is original, new, creative, and yet historical.

much like what happens when a DJ starts spinning and then opens up the microphone for a freestyle session.[6] Invariably, when one tries to listen to a freestyle, there is a line that isn't quite understood and can never be repeated in the way it was originally delivered. This is hip-hop: it is original, new, creative, and yet historical. As you listen to this edited freestyle of the history of the culture, you will notice that parts are mixed, missed, and not given the attention they deserve. It is up to those who bob their heads to the beat to input their voices and be a part of the remix. Here we go, my remix of hip-hop history.

Track 1: Who Is Yo' Baby's Daddy?

Hip-hop begins with the DJ. When I close my eyes and bounce to the opening of a hip-hop song, the first thing I do is think about the DJ who dropped that beat. There is power in that beat that demands my immediate affirmation. In their book *Yes Yes Y'all*, Jim Fricke and Charlie Ahearn[7] point us to the central role of the DJ, turned emcee, turned producer, turned fashion mogul, turned CEO, turned turntablist, who has to be credited with being at the birth of hip-hop. While I will argue in the next chapter that hip-hop, specifically rap music, is a child of the blues, there is a rough birth date or birth period for hip-hop culture. Fricke and Ahearn cite Ishmael Reed as the doctor who announced that a child was born by the name of hip-hop culture:

> *Hip-hop culture is a child of the city, specifically ethnic-minority, working-class communities.*

> In Ishmael Reed's brilliant 1972 novel *Mumbo Jumbo*, he writes of an African-inspired rhythmic virus that rises to battle the rigid forces of Western orthodoxy. Unknown to all but a small percentage of New Yorkers, hip-hop "jes grew" in the damaged, insecure city of my youth, and neither poverty nor indifference nor racism could stop it. In fact, to some degree all those things helped it grow."[8]

The birth certificate for hip-hop culture is dated 1972. It was the end of the Nixon administration, and though at the time we didn't know it, America was soon going to be looking the Carter administration in the face. Before we blinked, the Reagan years were upon us.

Fricke and Ahearn identify the birth of hip-hop culture as an inner-city phenomenon. Hip-hop culture is a child of the city, specifically ethnic-minority, working-class communities. Fricke and Ahearn put it this way:

> Hip-hop culture rose out of the gang-dominated street culture, and aspects of the gangs are still defining features of hip-hop—particularly territorialism and the tradition of battling. As hip-hop grew in the '70s, prominent DJs fathered the movement. The

DJs claimed specific territories as their own, and "crews" that derived either directly or in spirit from street gangs guarded the DJs, their equipment, and their territories.[9]

This was the birth of hip-hop families, and what started as territories would grow up to produce hip-hop culture nationally and internationally.

Three DJs were the early fathers of hip-hop culture: DJ Kool Herc, Afrika Bambaataa, and Grandmaster Flash.[10] Each of these DJs epitomizes hip-hop culture and the traits that Fricke and Ahearn cite as foundational at its beginning. They were connected to turfs, and in the case of Afrika Bambaataa, there was a connection to gangs. Grandmaster Flash developed a crew that was affectionately called Grandmaster Flash and the Furious Five. DJ Kool Herc had the Herculords, and Afrika Bambaataa had the Zulu Nation. James Brown, Gil Scott-Heron, and the Last Poets could be considered the forefathers of hip-hop, or rap poetry to beats, but hip-hop culture proper has as its birth parents these three DJs. These men are considered the fathers of hip-hop culture because at the base of the culture is the turntable. Turntables serve as the platform for the jump off.[11] We say the turntable, the instrument that produces the music, is the jump off because it provides that beat you hear first, before the rapper, or dancer, gets on. It is the beat that produces that move in our spirits that we can't quite explain.

Afrika Bambaataa: the spiritual father of hip-hop

So we ask the question, who is yo' baby's daddy? In the case of hip-hop, the baby's daddy is two turntables that were put side by side. It was on two turntables that the DJ began to play music that hadn't been played the way they were playing it or mixing it before. DJ Kool Herc, who is considered first out of the box, said that his formula was simple. He wanted to have parties and see people have a good time. His major contribution to hip-hop was his creativity in finding unique records and playing them for partygoers. He was famous for playing what was *not* being played on the radio. This was important for the growth, development, and attractiveness of hip-hop. Hip-hop set the standard; it didn't go with the flow. It was founded on rebelling against the mainstream. DJ Kool Herc said, "I was just the guy who played straight-up music that the radio don't play, that they should be playin', and people was havin' fun. Those records, people walk from miles around to get 'em 'cause they couldn't get 'em, they wasn't out there no more. 'Just Begun,' Rare Earth, James Brown, the Isley Brothers—they just love it. Ya Know."[12] Kool Herc found music that made people move. He was a digger, meaning he waded through old music and introduced it to a new audience in a new way. He was famous for throwing parties that were full of fun and rare music that made people dance.

DJ Kool Herc set the standard for creativity, and hip-hop culture followed suit. Doing things its own way is what made hip-hop unique. Hip-hop said, "Take us as we are, minority working class and all. We don't play what the radio plays. We aren't DJs for hire; we plan our own parties, design, print, and pass out our own flyers to promote our parties." When you see flyers from this early period—the late 1970s—you see the style of hip-hop culture emerging. The flyers have the flare, color, and boldness of graffiti. Hip-hop took nothing and made something out of it.

DJ Kool Herc started having parties and charging twenty-five cents for admission. This was basic street entrepreneurialism. Herc became so popular that break dancers were drawn to him. He introduced the b-boys and b-girls at his parties and encouraged their spirited free dancing. The Five Percenters, an offshoot of the Nation of Islam, became his peace guards, a group that maintained peace at parties.[13] Herc wasn't into gangs; he was into having fun. The elements of the culture were emerging around Herc: graffiti, street entrepreneurialism, break dancing, DJing, and emceeing. Hip-hop's popularity, realness, and connection to the streets fed its growth and development.

Track 2: Is That Baby Walking?

In Afrika Bambaataa we see the next growth period of hip-hop culture. Afrika Bambaataa, like DJ Kool Herc, didn't see the need to repeat what the radio was playing. Bambaataa saw war in the streets. The music on the radio wasn't bringing people in the inner city together. In an effort to promote peace, Bambaataa started the Zulu Nation. The Zulu Nation was a collective that centered on hip-hop culture for the purpose of bringing the warring gang factions together.

In the spirit of hip-hop, Bambaataa was creative; he took nothing and made something out of it as he started experimenting with sounds. He took the sounds of Kraftwerk,[14] a German techno group, and infused them into hip-hop. The combination of funk, rhythm and blues, and now techno created a foundation for the evolution of hip-hop. The principle here is as important as the action. Hip-hop brings people together across racial lines, and this started at its birth. There was no respect for racial barriers. And just as hip-hop brought working-class African Americans and Latinos together, it also brought German techno, rhythm and blues, and funk together. Bambaataa is considered the spiritual father of hip-hop.[15] He understood and promoted the spirit of coming together. This was an intentional act on his part. When I go to a hip-hop concert today, I see all shades, ages, and genders; this is no accident. It is a part of the founding heritage of hip-hop. DJ Kool Herc set the foundation, and Bambaataa extended that foundation to be intentionally inclusive.

From DJ Kool Herc, the founder, to Bambaataa, the spiritual father of hip-hop, we now reach Grandmaster Flash, the technical wizard of hip-hop. For hip-hop to bring it all together in the mix, there had to be a way to mix two records seamlessly. To mix records is to move from one song to the next as you are DJing a party while the dancers continue to dance. A seamless mix is when the dancers don't miss a beat as the DJ moves from one song to the next. The songs appear to blend into each other as they are mixed. Prior to Grandmaster Flash, DJs weren't mixing records seamlessly.

While DJ Kool Herc was experimenting with obscure artists and forgotten records and Bambaataa was focusing on the spiritual power in hip-hop to build community, there was yet to emerge a technician who could facilitate the process of the mix. Grandmaster Flash was a technical-school student who saw the need for what he would call a peekaboo system, which allowed the DJ to perfectly cue up or prepare the next song for the audience to hear. It would also allow the DJ to extend the good part, or breakdown part, of the record. DJs understood that there was a part of every song that the dancers went wild on, and DJs wanted to extend that portion of the song. Grandmaster Flash's peekaboo system was the answer. He designed a system that enabled the DJ to hear the next song or breakdown portion of the song and line them up and bring the next song in without the dancers noticing the change; it would blend right in. This was a key creative bridge for hip-hop. The mix became literally an act of bridging pieces of music, but it was also symbolic. Over the next twenty-five years, hip-hop would bring all kinds of music and people together.

Grandmaster Flash put it this way:

> My electronic knowledge had to come into play. I had to build these small amplifiers to drive the headphones, and then I would put these on the mixers. I had to create a "peek-a-boo" system. It allowed me to pre-hear the music in my ear before I push it out to the people. And what it involved was a switch attached to an external two- or

three-watt amplifier on the outside of the mixer, just enough to drive the headphones. Once I came up with the peek-a-boo system and I was able to pre-hear and take these five-second drum breaks and kind of segue them all together, then I just went out and just got "x" amount of duplicate copies of hot records and played the break. I would cut the break and then, with the duplicate copy, cut the break again to just keep it going. . . . Now I was able to play the break of all these songs in succession, back to back.[16]

This was a major development in hip-hop culture. It was larger than the music or the technical innovation. It signaled a key principle that has survived in hip-hop: putting things together that were historically separate. Breakdown portions of songs weren't meant to be heard together in loops. Instead, songs were structured in such a way that they progressed to the breakdown portion. Hip-hop looped them and connected them. This was hip-hop's creative spirit at work. It was a spirit of bringing things together and using sounds in a way they weren't intended to be used.

Track 3: So What Yo' Baby Say?

The turntable became an instrument in hip-hop as the DJ created new music by manipulating prerecorded music and sounds. The turntable was also a symbol of the old made new as old equipment was touched by young hands. These hands that touched the vinyl records and put the needles down on them were making a revolution (pun intended). As the records turned, hip-hop was re-evolving. Ironically, the next major development in hip-hop came when the record stopped.

A key in the arsenal of the hip-hop DJ was his or her ability to manipulate a record. They had to be able to drop the needle in the exact place that a sound started. This took precision and practice. They had to mark their records and know their marks. The next major development, the scratch (the moving of a record back and forth to get a hiss sound), was discovered or invented in a practice session. The DJs in this era were young and tended to live at home with their parents. The DJ Grand Wizard Theodore was practicing in his bedroom, and his mom came in and told him to turn his music down. He put his hand on the record to stop it while he was making a tape. Then, "when she left the room, I thought about what I was doing; I was trying to make a tape and I was like, wow, this really sounds like something."[17] Instead of rejecting the sound, Grand Wizard Theodore saw that he had something. The scratch was born.

The scratch—now famous in hip-hop—still consists of moving a record back and forth to make a noise like a hiss or a scratch. On Herbie Hancock's song "Rock It," the scratch became internationally famous. What makes the embrace of this discovery so hip-hop was hip-hop's embrace of what was never to be done. Vinyl records were never meant to be stopped and certainly not scratched.

I remember as a boy listening to records, the one thing you didn't want was a scratch on your record. We never touched the record, and we sure didn't stop it midrevolution to make a sound. When Grand Wizard Theodore stopped the record, the role of the DJ morphed into that of the producer, whose creative spirit involved doing what wasn't supposed to be done.

As hip-hop culture developed, the DJ's role of music creator remained constant. But the next development was the change in the role of the DJ from record/music man or woman to emcee. The father of hip-hop wasn't a rapper. DJ Kool Herc would talk a little, but he wasn't a rapper, or emcee, as we now call them. Grandmaster Flash remembers, "The Kool Herc style at the time was basically freelance talking, not necessarily syncopated to the beat. The three of them—Cowboy, Creole, and Mel [early emcees]—came up with this style called the back and forth, where they would be MC-ing to the beat that would play."[18] The DJ would say the first half of a sentence, and then the emcee would finish the sentence. This was what came to be called the back and forth method, or what is known in the black church experience as the call and response. The use of familiar sentences from nursery rhymes or common street sayings also got the crowd involved because members could join in the response. From the beginning, hip-hop was about getting the crowd involved. When I go to concerts today, the crowd is involved. We are encouraged to be a part of the show as we rap the choruses together, and many of the hardcore fans repeat every line to every song. While music fans may sing along to other genres, in hip-hop the mic is turned toward the audience. Audience members are expected to be a part of the show.

Track 4: Everybody in the House Say Ahhhh

As the DJ became the emcee, this second role became a part of the developing hip-hop culture. If you weren't efficient on the turntables, you could still be a major part of the show. Early emcees like Cowboy and Melle Mel performed with Grandmaster Flash. "With the emergence of first Cowboy and soon after Melle Mel and Kid Creole, the Bronx street scene was developing a distinctive style of MC-ing. But a smoother style of rapping DJ presided over the turntables in the clubs of Harlem and the Bronx. The style of DJs like DJ Hollywood and Eddie Cheba was closely tied to the mellow vocalizing of radio DJs like Jocko Henderson."[19]

As the emcee's role evolved, the various styles were linked to sets in New York. From the very start, the style of the emcee was linked to space or territory. As Murray Forman puts it, "Rap music takes the city and its multiple spaces as the foundation of its cultural production."[20] As the culture matured, the style of emceeing continued to be distinctive based on geography. Once again, let me emphasize that hip-hop culture was developing around the role of music. The style of rapping, dress, bravado, look, and talk were expressed in the various sets—or areas—of New York. The flyers that utilized graffiti-style art, which would later translate into album covers, were all a part of this process. The emcee set the stage for how hip-hop looked—what it wore, how it walked, how it talked. The emcee was out front, and everybody was taking notice.

The emcee moved from behind the turntables out to the front with a microphone in hand. It was the Funky 4, who would later become the Funky 4 + 1, who set the stage. DJ Jazzy Dee remembers, "The Funky 4 was the first ones that used mic stands in front of DJs. All the MCs used to stand back behind the DJ; I brung out four mic stands, and I put them out in the front of the DJs."[21] As the DJ moved to the background and mixed the records, the emcee moved to the front to control and lead the crowd. This wasn't a passing historical moment; it is pivotal in the culture. As the culture grew up, the DJ moved further to the background, while the emcee was elevated as the visible leader in the culture. The foundation of hip-hop was collective parties led by a DJ. Now the emcee led the party. The dancers, along with graffiti art and the DJ, also eventually moved backstage as the emcee stepped up. Even today when you mention hip-hop, the first thing most people think of is a rapper or rap music. As the rapper/emcee took center stage, the rapped word began to embody the whole of the culture. The attention on the rapper and his or her words wasn't unwarranted attention. The rapper was worthy of center stage, for his or her words carried the culture. The culture was put in their mouths, and as Adam did with the animals in Genesis, they named those parts of the culture and gave definition to hip-hop. The power of the word in hip-hop culture can't be overstated.

The history of hip-hop now focused on the evolution of the emcee as leader of the culture. After the Funky 4 was pushed out front by DJ Jazzy Dee, other DJs got crews to rap with them. Teams moved from protecting and carrying the DJ's equipment to leading the party. Grandmaster Flash, the technical wizard of hip-hop, led the way with his crew, Grandmaster Flash and the Furious Five.

During the late 1970s, hip-hop culture, a street art birthed out of struggle—or, as Kurtis Blow would say, out of "Hard Times"—was getting national buzz. The engine of capitalism was beginning to take notice, and record executives began to see potential profits.

One of the first to notice the earning potential in hip-hop and believe in it enough to take a chance was Sylvia Robinson. She was influenced by her son Joe Jr. to look into hip-hop. She took a look as both a mother and a businesswoman. In the end, she believed in hip-hop so much that she started a special record label, Sugar Hill Records, named after a section of Harlem that was once a haven for African American musicians, artists, and creative types.[22] Robinson saw the power in the art and aesthetics of hip-hop as coming from the streets. She also saw the connection and extension of African American culture in hip-hop. As much as hip-hop today is a male-dominated culture, women were important in the infant stage of hip-hop culture. Hip-hop's birth on the national scene came through a mother who believed in the child of African American culture.

Track 5: That Baby Done Run in the Streets

Once exposed to the streets of capitalism, this child was destined to change. The mother of hip-hop introduced her child to the outside world—the world outside the streets of New York, which had cuddled, suckled, and raised hip-hop culture. Putting hip-hop culture in the hands of the outside world was bound to tamper with the innocence of the culture. A change took place in hip-hop at this point in its maturation, and we must pick up the needle from the record. With Sugar Hill Records' *Rapper's Delight*, hip-hop effectively came out of the ghetto. As much as some in the old school want to glamorize the period from the late 1970s to the late 1980s, this was the period of the culture's commercialization. The child who was once loved and nurtured by the purist was now prostituted by bidders who didn't respect, understand, or love the culture and saw it only as a means to make money. What was once a pure child of the creative genius of the African American community, in partnership with its Latino brothers and sisters, would never be again. As much as Sugar Hill Records must be credited with putting hip-hop in the mainstream, it must equally be blamed for exposing the baby to the streets.

Once this move occurred and record companies saw they could make money on hip-hop, the frenzy began. While the early artists saw their work as art and continued to spit rhymes that had made them famous in the streets, this changed over time as managers and marketing came into play. After 1979 and the success of the Sugarhill Gang's major record, other labels began to get in the game. The first major record label to throw its hat in the ring was Mercury Records, which became interested in a struggling independent label started by Russell Simmons and Rick Rubin called Def Jam Recordings.[23] In 1979, Kurtis Blow came out with *Christmas Rappin'*, and the record sold over six hundred thousand copies.

The industry realized that *Rapper's Delight*, which sold over two million copies, wasn't a fluke. There was a market for hip-hop. After *Christmas Rappin'*, Kurtis Blow signed with Mercury Records and went on tour with Blondie on her 1980s British tour. Blow released the single "The Breaks" in May of 1980, which became the first rap twelve-inch certified gold record. (*Christmas Rappin'* was the second.) "The Breaks" peaked at number four on the R & B charts. It peaked at number eighty-seven on the US pop charts and number forty-seven in the UK. The record went on to sell in the millions. The record sales and chart-climb throughout the world signaled what was happening with hip-hop; it was becoming a global phenomenon. As the early rappers were rapping about tales from the 'hood over powerful beats, many were dancing to a story that they may or may not have taken seriously. The world was listening in on a party that the record companies had invited them to, and they were willing to buy a record as the price of admission.

When you listen to the story in "The Breaks," what do you hear? As much as this is a fun song with a great beat, it is also about the breaks in life that are hard to deal with. The song references losing your job, being hurt in an intimate relationship, borrowing money and not being able to pay it back. While this became a party song, it is also laced with the pain and struggle of the inner city. The inner city and its pain were wrapped up in early hip-hop, and this continues in hip-hop today. As hip-hop culture was being commercialized, the emcees continued to rap about what they saw, heard, and felt. They told stories. As Tupac said, "Sometimes I'm the watcher, and sometimes I'm the participant, and sometimes it's allegories and fables that have an underlying theme, underscoring how the generation gap has grown more menacing."[24] This is the early story of hip-hop and how the truth in hip-hop is in the story. Joan Morgan put it this way: "Truth is what happens when your cumulative voices fill in the breaks, provide the remixes, and rework the chorus."[25] When hip-hop hit the national scene and the nation was coming out of the disco dance craze, hip-hop offered a dance music laced with stories of the streets.

Today when I hear critics of hip-hop focus on a few words or images, the first question I ask is, what story is the song telling? What is the story about? That is why it is so important in this work to spend time talking about the story of hip-hop.

One of the most powerful story images of the move from disco to hip-hop was the music video for "Rapper's Delight." You see the Sugarhill Gang in T-shirts and clothes that are reminiscent of the struggle of the inner city, with (white) dancers in front of them in traditional disco attire. This video was a historical account of the next wave of popular culture, as the 'hood style through hip-hop was invited into clubs around the world. The change was occurring, and hip-hop was about to take over. As DJ Khaled said years later, "We takin' over."

The question that continues to swirl around in my mind is whether the new consumers of hip-hop culture, who weren't from the inner city, were listening to the stories. Today when I hear critics of hip-hop focus on a few words or images, the first question I ask is, what story is the song telling? What is the story about? That is why it is so important in this work to spend time talking about the story of hip-hop. Since this chapter provides only a snapshot of the story, it is important that you go further and get acquainted with the story of hip-hop.

In the 1980s, the development of the hip-hop industry sped up, and hip-hop entered the movies. In 1981, indie filmmaker Charlie Ahearn (who would later write about hip-hop) produced the film *Wild Style*. The film hit the streets in 1983. The move to make hip-hop movies was now on. The story about the growth of hip-hop was now on the big screen, and truth mixed with fiction to tell the tale. As the story got larger, the fathers of hip-hop, who were the beat makers and master mixers, were replaced by drum machines, and the hip-hop video image began to emerge in 1982–83; 1979 seemed like a distant yesteryear. In reality, what we find is that in four years capitalism had caught up.

Run-D.M.C.: the group that pushed hip-hop mainstream

The forces in the capitalist commercial market had found a way to package hip-hop culture—colors, diversity, and all. With the emergence of the hip-hop music video and music channels, hip-hop was now for sale to the highest bidder. When Fab 5 Freddy connected with the industry, it resulted in an indigenous hip-hop cultural icon getting in bed with Blondie (a white artist from England). So not only had the drum machines and hip-hop video emerged, but now scalpers had entered the culture as well. Blondie produced and recorded the song "Rapture," and it was over. That song, whose video included all the elements of hip-hop as well as a racially diverse cast, set the international hip-hop industry in full motion. Blondie's "Rapture" would become the first hip-hop record to top both the US and UK record charts. Hip-hop then matured rapidly. Ironically, the core artists were still young African Americans, male and female, looking to live the American dream.

Track 6: I See You

The hip-hop industry took hip-hop culture and put it in front of the world via the hip-hop movie and the hip-hop video. From *Wild Style* in 1983 to *Style*

Wars in 1983 to *Beat Street* in 1984 to *Breakin'* and *Breakin' 2: Electric Boogaloo* in 1984 to *Krush Groove* in 1985 to *Jam on the Groove* in 1997, hip-hop is now on the small screen and the big screen. It has become the marketing tool it was designed to be. The indigenous inner-city artists and dreamers thought they were seeing their American dream come true. In reality, they were losing some of their control over the art form. From now on, the culture would be influenced by the desire to be marketable and sellable. What the music industry found out early on was that the hardness of hip-hop as it reflected the harshness of inner-city life was sellable. Kids were buying it in the UK and the US.

As stars began to emerge, there was none bigger in the early years of hip-hop than Run-D.M.C. While Run-D.M.C. is credited with helping hip-hop cross over to the mainstream, I beg to differ with this characterization. Hip-hop never really crossed over. Rather, in its own unique way, it invited others to "walk this way."

When Run-D.M.C. burst on the scene in the early 1980s, the world was already walking toward hip-hop. The movies along with the early hits had made an impact. The genius of Rick Rubin would usher in the Run-D.M.C. era of hip-hop. Rubin knew that rock 'n' roll was a part of African American cultural history, that whites gravitated to, and he knew that whites had to some extent participated in its growing popularity. He believed that using rock 'n' roll as a foundation for the work of Run-D.M.C. would benefit them. This was a gamble that paid off. Their first album, in 1984, announced who they were: *Run-D.M.C.* When Run-D.M.C. collaborated with Aerosmith on "Walk This Way" in 1986, they had already announced they were the kings of rock with their aptly named second album, *King of Rock*. Their three-year run from 1984 through 1986 took hip-hop from the exotic to the mainstream, as listeners began to come to hip-hop. Run-D.M.C. was the first hip-hop group to get major airtime on MTV. This was an important shift because these young men came from Hollis, Queens; they weren't from the South Bronx. They brought a middle-, working-class sensibility to hip-hop.

On their first album, as they announce who they are, we hear their story. On the opening cut, "Hard Times," they let the listener in on how they see hard times. Once again the story is central, as the young African American artist, the emcee, tells what he has lived through, witnessed, and shared. For Run-D.M.C., times are hard. This song warns that hard times are coming to your town. It tells the story of how hard you have to work to try to stay ahead of hard times. It tells how you're going to have to fight if you hope to make it in this life. The key is hard work, which will hopefully help you deal with hard times.

From "Hard Times" to "Sucker M.C.'s," Run-D.M.C. set themselves apart. On "Sucker M.C.'s," they talk about being educated and light skinned and about going to college but also about liking collard greens. In this story, they claim their middle-class status while also asserting their roots in African American culture. The announcement that they like collard greens is a code for African Americans that the music and lyrics are products of African American culture.

They tell other MCs that it isn't enough to have meaningless rhymes and chant hip-hop. Their rhymes have to make sense, and their nouns and verbs have to agree.

In the third major song from their debut album, "It's Like That," they return to themes of struggle. "It's Like That" is a story about how hard life is for so many in the inner city. Run-D.M.C. open the story by talking about record unemployment and how people are struggling. They talk about premature deaths. They don't understand these things, but they see them and are telling the story. People are working hard, but hard times still find a way to touch them. They are trying to make ends meet, but it ain't happenin'. They try to get to work any way they can: car, train, bus, or on foot. They have been told to work hard if they want to compete, but in the end, ends don't meet. They don't know why, but "it's like that and that's the way it is."

The group embraced their lower-middle-class background, but they still let us know they haven't been excused from hard times. They have lived them and been in conversation with the story of struggle. As much as their rhymes ride over the riffs of rock 'n' roll, they are not devoid of soul. The kings of rock didn't look like rock stars. They didn't look like dressed-up, costume-wearing Afrika Bambaataa or Grandmaster Flash and the Furious Five. These brothers looked like they had just walked in off the streets of New York and started to perform.

The groundbreaking aspect of Run-D.M.C.'s work is now taken for granted in hip-hop: linking the story of hip-hop with the products of hip-hop. When Run-D.M.C. recorded the song "My Adidas" for their third album, it was because they wore Adidas. The story of their shoes was that they liked them. They bought them from a local store, and those shoes took them all over the world. They weren't used for illegal gain. They made legal gain with them and even helped the poor as they wore their Adidas when they performed at the Live Aid concert. Even though they had risen to the top, they would not change their Adidas for a different shoe. Run-D.M.C.'s celebration of their Adidas and Lee Jeans started a connection between hip-hop and product.[26]

Eithne Quinn, professor at the University of Manchester, suggests in her book that West Coast hip-hop was always laced to products; this was the case only because it followed on the heels of what Run-D.M.C. introduced.[27] The story of hip-hop became incarnated in the look and dress of hip-hop. Run-D.M.C. say that they have at least fifty pairs of these shoes, and they have them in all colors. The shoes, hats, and pants were hip-hop. But the way you wore them also became hip-hop. The shoes were worn with no laces; the pants were a bit loose; the gold chain hung down low. (In 2006, Jibbs did the song "Do My Chain Hang Low.") By the time we get to 50 Cent in Vitamin Water commercials, some have forgotten where this came from, but the root was Run-D.M.C. "My Adidas" was Run-D.M.C.'s first top 10 R & B single. This song paved the way for the future of hip-hop and product association and made it possible for Run-D.M.C. to walk this way.

Track 7: "Walk This Way"

Run-D.M.C.'s third album was *Raising Hell*, and the cut "Walk This Way" went places no other hip-hop song had gone. "Walk This Way" reached Billboard's top ten, and in the fall of 1986, it peaked at number four and stayed on the chart for sixteen weeks. The album *Raising Hell* became the first rap album to reach number one on the R & B charts, the first to go multiplatinum, and the first to reach pop's top ten. Run-D.M.C. would grace the cover of *Rolling Stone*—yet another first in the life of hip-hop—in true hip-hop style, embracing the streets and culture that produced them. They were black, in black, reaching back to the roots of rock 'n' roll.

This album, which was coproduced by Rick Rubin and Russell Simmons, invited everybody to the hip-hop party, and it worked. It wasn't as if this album and its success came out of nowhere. The table had been set in 1979, and the speed and furor that surrounded the meteoric rise of hip-hop were fueled by dollars and sense (pun intended). Rubin and Simmons knew the market, the cultural line, and they walked that way and ran with the culture. As Run-D.M.C. walked that way and kicked in the door, the floodgates now opened both ways. Record companies were looking for artists, and grassroots artists were looking for contracts. This appeared to be a marriage made in heaven. While the haves and the have-nots were moving farther away from each other, the pain index of the 'hood could now be recorded, videoed, and sold. The bidding was on, and hip-hop was on the auction block.

Don't miss the pain index. The hell in the streets was rising; you could see the fallout in the streets all around hip-hop, as poverty was on the rise, gun violence was increasing, jobs were disappearing, public schools were increasingly being underfunded and understaffed. The political climate of the nation was becoming increasingly more conservative, and careers in hip-hop were shaky. Was this genre going to survive as the economy turned down? What was the future of hip-hop? Would it have a long life? Run-D.M.C., only two years after their record-setting album *Raising Hell*, were yesterday's news. The hip-hop industry was looking for what was next. What other stories of pain were out there that could be told and sold? From Run-D.M.C. to Boogie Down Productions to LL Cool J and eventually to the West Coast, hip-hop had been introduced to the record industry in 1979 and now had become full partners.

In 1985, as Run-D.M.C. was on their way up and down, the younger artists with a new creative edge were waiting in the wings. LL Cool J turned attention to relationships between men and women as a new theme in hip-hop stories. Kool Moe Dee was the precursor to LL Cool J, who replicated Moe Dee's aggressive stance and rap style. Big Daddy Kane, who was a contemporary of LL Cool J, was also a lover man. LL Cool J came out with radio-ready hip-hop. His first album, in 1985 (a Def Jam production; LL was signed by Rick Rubin), was *Radio*. LL Cool J perfected the hip-hop ballad and the call to all the ladies for love. His name—Ladies Love Cool James—says it all. LL found himself in mixed company during this time in the hip-hop story. While LL was coming up in the story, he was surrounded by KRS-One and Boogie Down Productions, Kool Moe Dee, Big Daddy Kane, and Public Enemy. And we can't forget that Salt-n-Pepa, the first major female group, burst on the scene at this time as well.

Salt-n-Pepa, like the Sugarhill Gang, was created by a manager. Just like members of the Sugarhill Gang, they had regular jobs. Cheryl "Salt" James and Sandy "Pepa" Denton were working at Sears when Cheryl's boyfriend asked them to rap on a song. The rest is history. Salt-n-Pepa, with their female DJ, Spinderella, opened doors for the female rappers who would follow them. They were also instrumental in helping hip-hop expand its pop crowd. Their presentation of the hip-hop story and culture was party-focused and fun like early hip-hop, and it attracted a diverse audience. Queen Latifah was a peer of Salt-n-Pepa, coming out with *All Hail the Queen* in 1989, and before the Queen there was MC Lyte, who came out with *Lyte as a Rock* in 1988. But all these women have to trace their roots to the likes of the Mercedes Ladies, Roxanne Shante, the Real Roxanne, and the countless other women who stepped to the mic in hip-hop.[28]

> There was a tension in hip-hop then just as there is now. There were those who saw hip-hop as a political vehicle from the streets meant to save the streets, and there were others who saw hip-hop as a means off the streets into the corporate suites.

While Big Daddy Kane was also dealing with the relationship theme, other groups were more politically conscious and activist minded. There was a tension in hip-hop then just as there is now. There were those who saw hip-hop as a political vehicle from the streets meant to save the streets, and there were others who saw hip-hop as a means off the streets into the corporate suites. We can see this tension in the way Nas proclaimed that hip-hop was dead and T.I. said help was on the way.[29] T.I. was the most commercially successful artist in 2006, and at the end of the year, Nas claimed that hip-hop—or real hip-hop—was dead. T.I. came back in 2007 and responded that he was the savior of hip-hop; it was not dead. Nas was the political rapper; T.I. was the commercially successful party rapper. This same debate took place early on in hip-hop. In 1987 Kool Moe Dee symbolically ran over LL's trademark Kangol hat (another product link) on the cover of his *How Ya Like Me Now* album. This was an affront to LL and his brand of hip-hop.

Track 8: It's Golden: Fight the Power

Some say the late 1980s and early 1990s was the golden age of hip-hop. Those who romanticize this period lift up the political-activist-minded groups while ignoring LL Cool J and others who were not considered political. The late 1980s saw the emergence of the new hip-hop movie. The classic was Spike Lee's *Do the Right Thing*. As hip-hop was speaking loud about being black and proud, a new story emerged from the West Coast. The West Coast story began to be told via what was to be called gangsta rap.

West Coast hip-hop culture was much different from East Coast hip-hop culture. The key differences were the dates of birth and their relationships with the record industry. While Sylvia Robinson was an innocent mother putting her children on the street, West Coast record industry veteran Jerry Heller had a much different approach. While Robinson was taking a chance on a good idea, Jerry Heller saw rock 'n' roll all over again. He said, "I came into the record business with the rise of British invasion rock in the early 1960s. I remember a lot of the music executives at that time had an attitude toward rock as if they were waiting for it to go away. They sniffed it like you would a bottle of bad milk. . . . It was the same with rap in the mid-eighties."[30] While others looked down on hip-hop as a passing fad, Heller was not like his other white brethren in the record executive suites. He saw dollars, as with rock 'n' roll, and he became a major investor and exploiter of hip-hop.

If hip-hop was introduced to America through *Rapper's Delight* and the emergence of Run-D.M.C., the West Coast period marks the time when hip-hop culture and the record industry collided. Here hip-hop became the medium for the painful stories of those in the West Coast gang culture. Ice-T has to be counted as one of the fathers of West Coast hip-hop culture. He is famous for saying that something was happening on the West Coast that wasn't true of the East Coast. The gang violence and police brutality (which was fully exposed with the Rodney King beating in 1992) were a part of the West Coast story that West Coast rappers felt compelled to tell. The East Coast was a party scene with break dancers and rap battles in which rappers would rhyme against each other; on the West Coast, the term *wild, wild West* was appropriate. The West Coast didn't have break dancers; it had Fred Berry and the lockers, dancers that represented the West. It didn't have battle rap; it had gangsta rap.

In 1988, N.W.A (Niggaz Wit Attitude) dropped the classic album *Straight Outta Compton*, and it is really at this point in hip-hop history that the West Coast received national attention from the hip-hop community. Jerry Heller and Eric "Eazy-E" Wright were the masterminds behind the exposure the group received. But more important than savvy marketing and a shocking name was that *Straight Outta Compton* told a story of what the group called "street knowledge." The story opens with them announcing who they are and where they are from: "Straight outta Compton crazy mother—— named Ice Cube from the gang called Niggaz Wit Attitudes." They were boys from the 'hood who had something to say, and they were going to say it with an attitude. The next logical question is, why did they have an attitude? They had an attitude because they had been abused by the police. They make it clear in the story that the police are a part of the problem. If the listener missed this in the opening song/ story, it came through loud and clear in the next cut, "F— tha Police." N.W.A saw themselves as a different kind of a gang, but they were a gang. They were a gang that was designated to be the storytellers of the pain that their brothers and sisters in the 'hood on the West Coast were going through.

Eithne Quinn's book *Nuthin' but a "G" Thang: The Culture and Commerce of Gangsta Rap* tells how this revolutionary story of exposing pain became a product for sale to the highest bidder. While Quinn's assessment of the commercialization of gangsta rap singled out what happened with West Coast hip-hop culture, the story wasn't unpredictable. Hip-hop culture was being bottled and sold in the early 1990s. Jerry Heller and others like him were now on board, and the days of the mid-1970s would never be again.[31] Much of the West Coast history is in the work of Too Short, Ice-T, N.W.A, Dr. Dre, Snoop Dogg, the Dogg Pound, Daz and Kurupt, and, of course, Ice Cube, especially after he left N.W.A. The work of these artists tells more about the culture than the books that are published on the topic. That is why I encourage you to become listeners, watchers, and participants in hip-hop culture. If you want to learn the story of West Coast hip-hop culture, listen to that story straight from those who tell the story in time and rhyme.

Photofest

Too Short: an important figure in West Coast hip-hop

Hip-hop then moved again. The Dirty South emerged with a bounce that was driven by the bass drum. Tamara Palmer, in her book *Country Fried Soul: Adventures in Dirty South Hip-Hop*, gives us a glimpse of the Dirty South story.

In the foreword to Palmer's book, David Banner, an emcee/producer/actor from Mississippi, describes the Dirty South story this way:

> If you listen to Southern music, it's the most honest music in the world. Because Southern rappers are the only people that can tell you that they're weak and still be the hardest rapper in the world. It's the same person who in one song can talk about God and talk about the club in the same sentence. And when people look at it they say that it's a contradiction, but it's actually not. It's true life. It's honest life, because half of the people who are in church on Sunday still smell like Hennessy from the night before. But we mean it and it's not a joke; it's how we live.[32]

This is the unique twist in the story that the Dirty South provided. It was a true southern brand of hip-hop that exposed the vulnerability of the artists. It was this unique combination of joy, pain, and honesty that truly made the southern brand of hip-hop unique. The South saw God in the music right away. The fathers and mothers of the South didn't discount the spiritual content or inspiration of their music. They embraced the spirit force and used it for their inspirational benefit.

The early leaders in the Dirty South movement were Master P (New Orleans) and 2 Live Crew (Miami by way of California). Then there was the national breakthrough from Atlanta. Out of Atlanta came Outkast, Goodie Mob and Cee Lo Green, Jazze Pha, T.I., and the entire So So Def movement with Jermaine Dupree, who discovered Kriss Kross. As Kriss Kross would say, "Jump, Jump"—that was the foundation on which the Dirty South was built. It was hard, bass-driven bounce music that was later perfected by Lil Jon. This music made people move, and in the case of Outkast and Goodie Mob, it also made people think. It was a soul-searching music that moved people from the inside out. Hip-hop culture made an inward turn when it went south, and the South intentionally brought something deeper out of hip-hop culture that spoke to the spirituality of the music.

One of the fathers of the Dirty South was Cee Lo Green. Ironically, Green was the son of preachers. His father died when he was young, and he lost his mother later in life. Green saw his role in hip-hop culture as a religious/spiritual role. He said, "I think my mother and father are both watching me and I am full of their spirit and intention. My mother told me that my father once said that I would have something very special to do with my life. And so it's a fulfillment of

The next logical question is, why did they have an attitude? They had an attitude because they had been abused by the police. They make it clear in the story that the police are a part of the problem. If the listener missed this in the opening song/story, it came through loud and clear in the next cut, "F——— tha Police."

prophecy, each day that goes by. I'm proud that I believe in God."[33] There is no question here. Green saw his role as a leader of the Dirty South rap world as a fulfillment of prophecy. This prophecy came from God through his father. When Goodie Mob came out with their first major release, *Soul Food*, in 1995, who could forget the album cover, with them praying, hands up, seeking direction from God. This was the Dirty South as led by the likes of Green.

Green went on to say that the Dirty South produced praise music in hip-hop culture, though not what church folk traditionally call praise music. Green contended that what he and artists like him did was use their gift of music to praise God because they believed God was in the music. Green said:

> I feel like I was thought about and called to speak. So more or less my music is the dance of deserving. That's what I call it. Trying to earn and deserve what God has given me, 'cos I truly don't know what I've done to have it. And so it's gospel because it's praise and I praise God for sparing me and giving me a clue, giving me an idea. So it is praise in that sense. And it is a sacrifice of wanting to be pleasing in the sight of my Maker. If anything, my music is between me and God, you know, and I guess people get a chance to bear witness to that relationship. I know that sounds pretty big but it's very simple for me.[34]

Green and his peers claimed the God-force in their music and their personal lives. They saw God as cocreator of hip-hop culture as it developed.

Interestingly, the tensions emerging in hip-hop culture were very much linked to the various regional developments. The forces of commercialization and commodification were coming out of the West, along with stories of pain and redemption. And then there came a force from the South that was intentionally linked to God consciousness and affirmation. N.W.A's attitude was reflected on their debut album cover as viewers looked down the barrel of a gun. At the same time, Goodie Mob's debut album showed palms uplifted in prayer. As they lifted their hands in prayer to God, they were simultaneously selling the culture. They were essentially "selling soul." Green exposed the tensions when he said, "I want to spread optimism and faith and hope with the medium of music. And so that's what the political stance and savvy comes from as well. I do believe there is an industrial genocide. I say this all the time but it never stops making sense that a capitalist society has to have somebody to capitalize on."[35] How do these artists who want to get their word out do it without using the distribution chains of the hip-hop industry? There were those who saw the exploitation of the culture, but they were still trying to appeal to the best of the culture while trying to participate in an economic system that was built on making a profit off someone or something. The development of hip-hop culture was now caught in the crossfire of Americana.

Hip-hop next emerged in the Midwest. The breakout group from the Midwest was Bone Thugs~n~Harmony, who were from Cleveland, but their albums were produced by Eazy-E of N.W.A and Ruthless Records. The influence of the West Coast sound can be heard in their music, but the lyrics and rapid-fire rap style were uniquely Midwestern. Bone Thugs~n~Harmony bridged the East and the West, and their song "Tha Crossroads" symbolized what they and the Midwest were to be to hip-hop culture. "Tha Crossroads" was a song that dealt with death and the afterlife. It was full of familiar religious imagery. I will never forget the first time I saw the video on BET. I was in our family room ironing clothes for my children, and I stopped midstream because the video was so powerful. There was even a closing scene in the video where the dead were taken to heaven. Here was the g-funk—or gangsta funk sound, that sound that had the organ as its base—of the West Coast and the religious and spiritual content of the Dirty South wrapped up in the fast-paced rap of the Midwest. Nelly and Twista would follow this style of fast-paced, Midwest rapping. From the Midwest, hip-hop traveled to the Third Coast.

Green and his peers claimed the God-force in their music and their personal lives. They saw God as cocreator of hip-hop culture as it developed.

The Third Coast is what you may know as Houston, Texas.[36] Mike Jones became the first of the Third Coast to go platinum. It was his 2005 album, *Who Is Mike Jones?* that made the breakthrough. That was when most of America heard about the candy paint (candy-colored cars), grillz (false teeth or gold teeth plastered across one mouth), and 84s (big tires on cars), but the foundation of the Third Coast predates Mike Jones's breakthrough. Twenty years before Mike Jones, J. Prince had a dream, and Prince's Rap-A-Lot Records laid the foundation for the empire we now know through Lil Flip, Lil Keke, UGK, Chamillionaire, Slim Thug, and Paul Wall. In the early 1990s, DJ Screw, a pioneer in Third Coast hip-hop, created a new sound by slowing the music down. Then Swisha House and Michael "5000" Watts took what DJ Screw invented and perfected it. But there wouldn't have been Third Coast national notoriety without Scarface and the Geto Boys.

The Geto Boys saw the light of day in 1986, but their contribution to the larger hip-hop culture was denied distribution because the same industry that produced the most violent movies in the world contended that their work was too graphic. Rick Rubin came to the rescue and arranged distribution through his own Def American label. The Geto Boys dropped *Makin' Trouble* in 1988, *Grip it! On That Other Level* in 1989, *The Geto Boys* in 1990, *We Can't Be Stopped* in 1991, *Uncut Dope: Geto Boys' Best* in 1992, and then a greatest hits album in 2002, all produced by Rap-A-Lot Records. The Geto Boys were the foundation of Third Coast hip-hop culture—a culture rooted in the nine thousand square miles that make up the Houston-Galveston-Brazoria Consolidated Metropolitan Statistical Area. An obsession with cars is expected in a place so large. So Third Coast hip-hop slowed the music down to make the long rides mellow.

Born in the USA

In America, hip-hop culture was birthed and developed in regional incubators: from the Northeast to the West Coast to the Dirty South to the Midwest and finally to the Third Coast. Hip-hop culture looks and sounds different in each region. These are hip-hop families, and each family had parents who birthed it and gave it a unique cultural imprint. But hip-hop didn't stop in the United States; hip-hop has become an international phenomenon. This morning, as I was preparing for my morning run, I was watching the Black Eyed Peas perform before a sold-out audience in Sydney, Australia. The book *Global Noise*, edited by Tony Mitchell, testifies to the international expansion of hip-hop culture. Mitchell says, "Hip-hop and rap cannot be viewed simply as an expression of African American culture; it has become a vehicle for global youth affiliations and a tool for reworking local identity all over the world."[37]

If Mitchell and his team of writers don't convince you that hip-hop has gone global, read *Hip-Hop Japan: Rap and the Paths of Cultural Globalization* by Ian Condry. He contends that hip-hop has spread around the world:

> Hip-hop caught on because it spread through the smoky bowels of Tokyo's underground club scene. There one can experience the ways Japanese hip-hop draws inspiration from American artists while at the same time integrating the language and everyday understandings of Japanese youth. . . . Hip-hop [is a revolution in Japan] because it [provides] a particular means for youth to express themselves.[38]

In the context of Japan, we see hip-hop once again taking on a regional flavor as another child of hip-hop culture is born. Young people are empowered to share their stories with their peers, in their language, in their unique medium of communication. They rap hip-hop and dress hip-hop because they are hip-hop.

What I have presented here is only a snapshot of hip-hop history. Another way to grasp the history of hip-hop is to engage the culture. As much as I would argue that a growing part of the culture can be seen in books like this one, nothing beats exploring the culture itself. So you are not done; go and engage the culture. The resources listed below will help you do just that.

Getting in Touch with Hip-Hop

Sistas on the Mic

Hill, Lauryn. *The Miseducation of Lauryn Hill*. Ruffhouse/Columbia, 1998.
MC Lyte. *Lyte as a Rock*. First Priority/Atlantic, 1988.
Queen Latifah. *All Hail the Queen*. Tommy Boy, 1989.

Salt-n-Pepa. *Hot, Cool, and Vicious*. Next Plateau, 1986.

Yo-Yo. *Make Way for the Motherlode*. East West/Atlantic, 1991.

East Coast Hip-Hop Albums

Afrika Bambaataa and Soulsonic Force. *Looking for the Perfect Beat*. Tommy Boy, 1983.

Blow, Kurtis. *Kurtis Blow*. Mercury, 1980.

Boogie Down Productions. *Criminal Minded*. B-Boy, 1987.

Fat Boys, The. *The Fat Boys*. Sutra, 1984.

Public Enemy. *It Takes a Nation of Millions to Hold Us Back*. Def Jam, 1988.

West Coast Hip-Hop Albums

Dr. Dre. *The Chronic*. Death Row, 1992.

Ice Cube. *Death Certificate*. Priority, 1991.

Ice-T. *Rhyme Pays*. Sire/Warner Bros., 1987.

N.W.A. *Straight Outta Compton*. Ruthless, 1988.

2Pac. *2Pacalypse Now*. Jive, 1991.

Dirty South Hip-Hop Albums

Goodie Mob. *Soul Food*. LaFace, 1995.

Kriss Kross. *Totally Krossed Out*. Ruffhouse/Columbia, 1992.

Master P. *The Ghetto's Tryin to Kill Me!* No Limit, 1994.

Outkast. *Southernplayalisticadillacmuzik*. LaFace, 1994.

2 Live Crew. *As Nasty as They Wanna Be*. Luke Skywalker, 1989.

Midwest Hip-Hop Albums

Bone Thugs~n~Harmony. *E 1999 Eternal*. Ruthless, 1995.

Common Sense. *Can I Borrow a Dollar?* Relativity, 1992.

Nelly. *Nellyville*. Universal, 2002.

West, Kanye. *The College Dropout*. Roc-A-Fella, 2004.

Third Coast Hip-Hop Albums

Geto Boys. *The Geto Boys*. Def American, 1990.

Jones, Mike. *Who Is Mike Jones?* Warner Bros., 2005.

Slim Thug. *Already Platinum*. Geffen, 2005.

Books

Chang, Jeff. *Can't Stop, Won't Stop: A History of the Hip-Hop Generation*. New York: St. Martin's Press, 2005.

Fricke, Jim, and Charlie Ahearn. *Yes Yes Y'All: The Experience Music Project Oral History of Hip-Hop's First Decade*. Cambridge, MA: Da Capo Press, 2002.

Ogg, Alex, and David Upshal. *The Hip-Hop Years: A History of Rap*. New York: Fromm International, 2001.

Toop, David. *The Rap Attack: African Jive to New York Hip-Hop*. Boston: South End Press, 1984.

———. *Rap Attack 2: African Rap to Global Hip-Hop*. London: Serpent's Tail, 1994.

———. *Rap Attack 3: African Rap to Global Hip-Hop*. London: Serpent's Tail, 2000.

VIBE Books. *Hip-Hop Divas*. New York: Three Rivers Press, 2001.

r u still down?

Hip-Hop Culture as an Extension
of the Blues

The words of Jeremiah son of Hilkiah, one of the priests at Anathoth in the territory of Benjamin. The word of the LORD came to him in the thirteenth year of the reign of Josiah son of Amon king of Judah, and through the reign of Jehoiakim son of Josiah king of Judah, down to the fifth month of the eleventh year of Zedekiah son of Josiah king of Judah, when the people of Jerusalem went into exile.

The word of the LORD came to me, saying,

"Before I formed you in the womb I knew you,
    before you were born I set you apart;
    I appointed you as a prophet to the nations."

"Ah, Sovereign LORD," I said, "I do not know how to speak; I am only a child."

But the LORD said to me, "Do not say, 'I am only a child.' You must go to everyone I send you to and say whatever I command you. Do not be afraid of them, for I am with you and will rescue you," declares the LORD.

Then the LORD reached out his hand and touched my mouth and said to me, "Now, I have put my words in your mouth. See, today I appoint you over nations and kingdoms to uproot and tear down, to destroy and overthrow, to build and to plant."

Jeremiah 1:1–10

It's like a jungle sometimes it makes me wonder how I keep from going under.

Grandmaster Flash and the Furious Five

Track 1: Hip-Hop as a Lament

The weeping prophet Jeremiah greets us as we begin our journey into the world of hip-hop. Why do we start with Jeremiah? We start with Jeremiah because when I listen to hip-hop I hear the pain, suffering, and cry from the culture. As I listened to CD after CD, I had an ear-opening experience. It sounded as if there were a cry masked by the hard veneer and tattooed bodies of the artists. At the same time, I was reading Jeremiah in my devotional time. Then it hit me: the writing of Jeremiah and the lyrics sounded alike. They collaborated in my spiritual journey as I sought to understand Jeremiah and hip-hop. Hip-hop and Jeremiah began to shed light on each other. I began to wonder, what if we heard hip-hop as the voice of a weeping prophet? What if we heard hip-hop artists as hurting and oppressed people called by God, being used by God to speak?

We start with Jeremiah because when I listen to hip-hop I hear the pain, suffering, and cry from the culture.

Hip-hop artists are typically young, like Jeremiah. Young people often question their purpose and what they are called to do and be. Rappers and the members of the hip-hop nation, like Jeremiah, are trying to find their way. As they do, they speak of their pain and the pain of their followers while simultaneously speaking prophetically. This pain is one of wrestling for identity and self-definition in opposition to a dominant culture that uses them, their art, and their voices while not fully affirming or celebrating who they are.

Maybe they have heard God and are not afraid. Maybe they trust in God and use their mouths to uproot and tear down, to destroy and overthrow, to build and to plant. What if God is actually using hip-hop and its young artists to speak prophetically to the church and call her to task? What if we listened to hip-hop as we would a prophet? What would we hear? What would we see? How would we react? How would it change our relationship with hip-hop? When I see hip-hop as a young prophet, I hear something different. I hear something different because I am listening differently. Stop, look, and listen with me.

The quest we are on as we engage hip-hop culture is to find God. Is God in hip-hop culture? If so, where is God? How is God using the message and meaning in hip-hop culture to share his Word and wisdom with the world? If we come to hip-hop looking for a word from God through a weeping prophet, we will be better situated to hear the meaning in the message that is wrapped up in the narratives of hip-hop. Maybe, just maybe, hip-hop is a lament. This lament is one of searching that is linked to a critique of the old as the young seek to find meaning in their religious and spiritual quest.

The language of the young is idealistic and sometimes fatalistic. Hope is caught in a paradox. Young adults are locked in the middle, not quite their parents' peers and yet removed from the nonchalant teenage years. They say and do things they may later regret, but they produce and drive change in a culture because they are risk takers; they aren't afraid to speak their minds. They speak truth as they see it, live it, and know it. The young shout from the mountaintops, and this is exactly what hip-hop does. It is a world of prophetic engagement. Let him or her who has ears hear what the hip-hop prophets are saying to us!

Track 2: The Roots and Contextualization of the Message in "The Message": The Story and Storyteller

Hip-hop is a child of the city. Young prophets cry out as they live in a world that those who could escape have escaped. African American youth and young adults face what appear to be hopeless odds, and they fight back through the prophetic arm of hip-hop. The struggle and roots of hip-hop come to life in the music, lyrics, and culture that is hip-hop. A classic song that is an archetype of the prophetic in hip-hop is "The Message" by Grandmaster Flash and the Furious Five. As you eavesdrop on the message in "The Message," you see, hear, and feel the power in hip-hop and its ability to create a prophetic, redemptive, healing space. Joan Morgan says, "Though it's often portrayed as part of the problem, rap music is essential to that struggle because it takes us straight to the battlefield. . . . I believe hip-hop can help us win. . . . The information we amass can help create a redemptive, healing space for brothers and sistas."[1]

The message in hip-hop is rooted in the stories or narratives that emcees weave on top of beats that are laid down by DJs as they take us to the battlefield of the inner city. The story and struggle of inner-city life are played out via songs and the lived stories of both the artists and the members of the hip-hop nation. The hip-hop nation is made up of those who subscribe to hip-hop culture as a way of life. They see themselves as hip-hop and proclaim hip-hop culture as a central component of their identity. Their life story is somehow shaped by and connected to the story of and in hip-hop.

I encourage you to listen to the message in hip-hop. We have to stop, look, and listen for the story. What are the artists trying to say? What is the message in their story? As twisted as some might feel their story is, it is still their story. It may or may not be a true story; it may be based on a true story. Either way, there is truth in the story. In the story is the message, and in the message we will find the redemptive principles and properties of hip-hop.

In hip-hop, the rapper or emcee becomes the chief storyteller, as his or her rhymes ride over the beats that move the spirits and affect the emotions of the listeners. The beat calls for the instant affirmation by the nodding of the head, and then comes the emcee/storyteller. Will Coleman says, "Rappers are the contemporary *griots*, the contemporary storytellers. They come out of a tradition that goes back to gospels, spirituals, blues, jazz, R&B, and now rap. It's all a part of that same 'tribal talk.'"[2] Stic.man, of the rap duo Dead Preze, wrote in his book *The Art of Emceeing* that

> an emcee is a creator, innovator, communicator, orator, translator, teacher, visionary, representative, thinker, convincer, speaker, storyteller, messenger, poet, griot, a writer, master of ceremonies, historian, leader, reporter, a vocal instrument, philosopher, fan, an observer, a student, therapist, social analyst, evangelist, a minister, professor, sales person, motivator, mack, charmer, host, and artist all in one![3]

As the emcee lives out the call to be what Stic.man has defined an emcee to be, he or she does so in concert with the crowd of listeners who become cocreators and re-creators of the rhyme as they experience what they hear as the beat moves their spirits along. The truth and power of hip-hop are as much in the rhyme as in the beat. Coleman goes on to talk about the story in African American culture, which is rooted in "emplotment" and "narrativity":

> Emplotment is the arrangement of heterogeneous factors (events, circumstances, characters, and so on) into meaningful thought patterns that tell a story. . . . Narrativity, though closely associated with emplotment, relates more to the overall effect of a text as a literary genre. It encompasses the entire spectrum of semantic codes that are incorporated into the development of a plot—that is, it develops and carries the story from beginning to end.[4]

To understand the message in "The Message," we must employ the tools of emplotment and narrativity analysis as we look for the arrangement of the events, circumstances, and characters involved in the song. We must then ask questions about the codes that are used in the song along with the plot that is developed and that carries the story from beginning to end.

The redemptive principle in hip-hop is rooted in the truth in the stories that artists tell as they resonate with both their own lived experience and that of their listeners. It is the lived, historical experience that makes hip-hop truthful. Joan Morgan explains, "Truth is what happens when your cumulative voices fill in the breaks, provide the remixes, and rework the chorus."[5] The truth in and of hip-hop is about the rapper and the story as well as those who appropriate the message. This is the process of the remix. James Cone put it this way in regard to the blues:

> Historical experience, as interpreted by the black community, is the key to an understanding of the blues. Black people accepted the dictum: Truth is experience, and experience is the Truth. If it is lived and encountered, then it is real. There is no attempt in the blues to make philosophical distinctions between divine and human truth. That is why many blues people reject the contention that blues are vulgar or dirty.[6]

Hip-hop shares this principle of truth. In hip-hop, truth is told, lived, and defined, and therefore hip-hop music is about truth. Whether or not the artist himself lived what he is rapping about is important, but it is not as important as the truth in the lyrics. Listeners resonate with that truth and are freed and affirmed when they hear their story spoken aloud. The story that is spoken may not be an accurate retelling of their lives, but there is some truth in the story that excites and touches them, and as a result they are moved. As hip-hop truth/theological reflection is pieced together over the beats, a liberating voice emerges. Hip-hop is not one voice or one truth, but many. According to Will Coleman, "Many voices speaking at the same time, from different, even conflictive, perspectives, nevertheless also constitute a 'beat' or voice-story about African and African American way of being, knowing, and living. Each beat is distinct as it contributes to the overall cadence of coming into being."[7] Hip-hop and the stories it weaves and tells are the coming together of lives, stories, and truth. Hip-hop becomes a way of being, knowing, and living.

Track 3: The Message in Hip-Hop Is "The Message": What Is the Message in "The Message"?

"The Message" contains different voices rapping over a beat testifying to the truth in lived experience. When you listen to Grandmaster Flash and the Furious Five's song "The Message," what do you hear? What do you feel? What do you see? Let me share how I experience the truth in this song. I say *experience* because when I come to hip-hop I am not simply a listener. I actually experience something as the beat drops and my mind and body immediately respond. I begin to nod my head and tap my feet as the song invites me into the story.

"The Message" opens with an extended musical intro. The song is 7 minutes, 13 seconds long. As the intro opens, there is a heavy beat of the kick drum doubling up. The beat calls for the immediate affirmation that hip-hop demands: the head nod. Then you hear the signature synthesizer crying as the song continues. The chorus begins, "It's like a jungle sometimes." This opening image drives the song verbally, visually, and experientially. The video that complements the song opens with scenes from the inner city; the song is set in inner-city New York.

The redemptive principle in hip-hop is rooted in the truth in the stories that artists tell as they resonate with both their own lived experience and that of their listeners.

While calling this place a jungle and pointing to its harsh living conditions, the writer of the song voices his amazement that he hasn't gone over the edge as a result of these oppressive conditions. He says, "It makes me wonder how I keep from going under." The statement is a question, a critique, and a cry all in one.

The truth of the song is captured in the context of the rough living conditions, which are not just the struggle of the lead rapper in the song; this song is also about a man, his wife, his brother, his mother, and the children of the community. The song tells the story of what the city has done to them, how these oppressive living conditions have adversely affected their chances. In essence, the rapper is rapping about or telling the story that sociologists like William J. Wilson researched and wrote about during this same era.[8]

As the song moves from the chorus, the first verse opens with the sound of a bottle shattering. In the video, the bottle falls to the ground and shatters. The first verse describes what the jungle looks like and feels like. It is an environment with broken glass, bad smells, and noise. The storyteller announces these conditions but then says he has no choice. He can't move out. He can't move out because he has no money. He also doesn't have a car; because of his lack of funds, his car has been repossessed. The video shows a tow truck waiting to do what it does. The setting for the story is set. We are in the jungle. The storyteller is locked in an environment where people's spirits have been broken and they find it difficult to care anymore.

The song moves right out of the verse into the chorus. There is no break in the song, no time to breathe. The chorus is different the second time around. Now that the setting has been set, the storyteller is more animated, more passionate about his pain. The chorus is altered in emotion, and the words are different. A line is added at the end of the first stanza in which the storyteller moans, "Uh huh ha ha ha." At first glance, this appears almost inconsequential, but it is meaningful. The storyteller is sharing a pain that can't be articulated. He is saying something that can't be said, and this becomes a way of crying out or weeping as others feel what he is saying. The line "Don't push me" is also added to this chorus. The storyteller is letting us know that he is so close to breaking because of his pain in the 'hood that he may go off. He can't take a touch or a push, because any additional pressure could push him over the edge. He is also implying that the reason so many people in the 'hood lose it is because they are being pushed by their circumstances.

Underneath his words is that famous repeated loop of kick drum and synthesizer. The drum is powerful throughout the song as it continues to call for a response. The bongo is heard after the kick drum, and then we hear the sounds of the street that support the setting of the story being lived, told, retold, interpreted, and felt by the artist and the listener. We become participants in the drama as the story pulls us in and we nod and lean. The musical track that the story rides on can't be ignored. This isn't just a poem that one is experiencing. This is a story that is equally music/track and lyric. The lyric doesn't work without the track, and the track doesn't work without the lyric. They are laid down together. They make an impact on the listeners as feelings and emotions are touched. One hears, sees, and feels as the two ride together, lyric and track.

As the song moves into the second verse, the character of interest has changed. The story now looks specifically at what the harsh conditions of the inner city have done to a once-vibrant young woman. The emcee puts himself in the role of observer looking out his window. He lets the listener in on what he sees. He sees a lady who has lost her mind. This woman moved to the city with big hopes. When she first arrived, she would call her friends back home and tell them about the life she was living. Before too long the city pushed her over the edge, and now she is a broken spirit. She went from being a beauty queen to being pimped. The city abused her and broke her, and now she is eating out of a garbage can. As the storyteller watches and reflects on her story, it is obvious that her story has affected him. He is moved by her tragic end. He can't ignore her presence in his world. As he ends the verse, he dips back into the chorus, and we hear that haunting, memorable line, "Don't push me 'cause I'm close to the edge." The line haunts you because the storyteller has just given an account of one who *was* pushed over the edge. You can hear his fear and vulnerability, as those he is watching are a reflection of his own struggles. Can the city do this to you?

In the third verse, the storyteller introduces his extended family. His brother is a victim of drug addiction and steals the television from their mother's home. The storyteller then invites us back into his immediate world as he reflects on his own financial struggles. Things have gotten so bad in his life that the bill collectors are hounding him and his wife. His wife has become anxious about the calls, and both of them feel paralyzed. They don't know what to do. His poor economic standing is linked to his poor education in public schools and double-digit inflation. His car has been repossessed, and now the train workers are on strike, so he can't even take the train to work. He cries out that the pressure is so intense that it feels like King Kong is standing on his back. He is so stressed that he fears he might go insane. He is even tempted to hijack a plane. The passion at the end of the verse is obvious. You can hear the constant worry in the storyteller's voice. He is close to the edge. As you feel this passion at the end of this verse, he begins the chorus, "Don't push me 'cause I'm close to the edge." As each verse gives way to the chorus, the edge that he warns of becomes more visible. You can see and feel what he is talking about.

Before the song transports the listener into the fourth verse, there is a pause. This chorus has no moan, no "uh huh," but the music is allowed to breathe and speak. As the track comes out of the chorus, the storyteller is silent. For sixteen bars the track speaks. The loop of bass drum and synthesizer keeps the listener engaged until the storyteller tells us about his son. His son has become cynical at a young age. He wonders aloud about the benefits of education. He is afraid to walk in the park in his own community; he has taken to carrying a gun and is contemplating dropping out of school and becoming a street sweeper or a part of the hip-hop industry. The boy sees America as a place that is all about money and cons. The son sees what the harsh conditions have done to his father, and now he wonders how he will survive in this world that pushes people to the edge. The boy is being tossed to and fro, from hope to hopelessness.

As the song moves back to the chorus after the fourth verse, we notice the chorus once again has changed. It has become a contemplative lament. Instead of twice repeating the phrase "it's like a jungle sometimes," the emcee says it four times. The voice is muted, as if the jungle is taking its toll on the storyteller. You can hear him wondering aloud, "I wonder how I keep from going under?" He is amazed that he is still alive.

The fifth verse, which foretells the future, moves from lament to the prophetic. The effects of the jungle are pressing not only the storyteller and his family but also others living in those same conditions. The prophet tells of the future while weeping about the outcome. He introduces us to a child who is born in the 'hood, or the jungle. This child doesn't know or understand what he is about to face. The storyteller cries out, "God is smilin' on you but he's frownin' too because only God knows what you'll go through." God is brought into the picture. God is concerned about the 'hood. As much as others may have turned a deaf ear, as much as it appears that no one cares, God does. Not only does God care, but God cries with them, God feels their pain, God sees what they are going through. Others frown on the poor with a spirit of judgment or sympathy. God's frown is one of empathy and compassion. Why is God frowning? What is the source of the pain?

The source of the pain is rooted in the truth of what poverty and hard times do to those who are stuck in the inner city trying to survive. The child in the inner city sees survival as choosing from limited options and opportunities. A second-rate education will not fully equip him to compete. Then there is the criminal activity that is allowed to prosper in his 'hood as governmental authorities turn the other way. The kid grows up and sees what the storyteller calls thugs, pimps, pushers, and big moneymakers. He infers that the kid will look up to them and want to grow up to be like them. When the kid makes his choice from his limited options for upward socioeconomic mobility, he drops out of high school and eventually goes to jail. The lifelong struggle has taken its toll on the now young adult. During his jail sentence, the child, all grown up, commits suicide. The pain outside and inside was too much for him. Death became a solution. The eight-year prison sentence was the straw that broke the young man's spirit, and his will to live. He, like the apostle Paul, struggled with life or death (Phil. 1:20–26), and he decided to choose death. While the entire song wrestles with being pushed over the edge, in this final verse, we see that these conditions can push you over the edge. This boy who grew up to become a young man was pushed over the edge. His life was lost.

What caused this young man's death? Did the boy commit suicide, or was he murdered? Are the conditions in the 'hood so oppressive that they actually push people over the edge? Are these conditions ignored by America, the richest country in the world? Are the American government and the American public accomplices to the deaths of the young inner-city residents? Does America see how inner-city residents are being pushed over the edge? While America dances to their lament, do they hear the cry? Are hip-hop artists crying out for help? Are they lamenting their conditions? As the verse ends, it bleeds into the chorus for the last time, where a subtle but powerful insertion has been made. As the storyteller introduces the chorus, he says, "So, don't push me cause I'm close to the edge." The introduction of the word *so* is an indication that when those in the inner city are pushed, the edge isn't far away. It also calls to mind how tender and fragile life is for those who are subjected to inner-city poverty. While many run around the inner city acting tough, in reality the toughness of the environment, or jungle, is enough to break them down. They are on the edge.

Are the conditions in the 'hood so oppressive that they actually push people over the edge? Are these conditions ignored by America, the richest country in the world? Are the American government and the American public accomplices to the deaths of the young inner-city residents?

What is the truth in this story? What do you hear? What do you feel each time you listen? Mack 10 said on his website, "The best music transports the listener to another world, a place where they can see, hear, touch, smell and imagine—all because of the music coming from their speakers."[9] What do you imagine as you hear the story of "The Message"? Are you transported by this classic? As the song closes, the rappers become a metaphor for the imprisonment they have rapped about. In the video, the group is arrested by the police. They loudly proclaim that they are with a rap group, Grandmaster Flash and the Furious Five, and the police ask if that is a gang. They tell them it is a rap group, but the police disregard their story and put them into a police car. The police not only ignore their claim of being a musical group but also remark, "You are the problem." African Americans and rappers are seen as creating the problem that "The Message" argues against. "The Message" tells us that they didn't create the problem, and they aren't the problem. Rather, they are victims of the injustice of an American system that pushes them to the edge and supports a class-based economic system of haves and have-nots.

Track 4: The Creation and the Ground of Hip-Hop: An Inner City Built on Inequity

Robin d.g. Kelley, in his book *Yo' Mama's Disfunktional*, says, "I wrote this book quite literally in defense of my own mother and my two sisters, all of whom have made valuable political contributions to the world we inhabit; and all of whom spent a brief moment of their lives on welfare."[10] What does Kelley mean by this statement? He means that when it comes to the inner city, the problem is reduced to poor parenting and limited by a wrongheaded self-help theory. Kelley exposes the limits of the self-help philosophy, and he also amplifies in his work what Grandmaster Flash and the Furious Five rapped about. Kelley sheds light on how hard inner-city African Americans work to survive on limited resources. The mothers in the 'hood are some of the hardest-working mothers in the world. The mothers in the 'hood aren't the problem, according to Kelley. Kelley points to a system of oppression that is built on and supported by a governmental system and an intellectual community that don't understand or want to be a part of liberating those who are caught in the jungle on which "The Message" sheds light. Kelley says, "Let us not forget that government policies, not black people's moral failings, are largely responsible for the current crisis. The Reagan/Bush revolution dismantled state protections for the poor, working people, people of color, and the environment; it expanded the urban police state; and it assembled a judiciary clearly more concerned with protecting capital than protecting the rights of ordinary citizens."[11] "The Message" told us the story of how people in the inner city were responding to what Kelley describes. When "The Message" hit the scene in 1982, the Reagan era was in full swing: social services were being undermined, the middle class was making their exodus from the inner city, and the jungle was being left behind.

The problems of the inner city evolved out of the creation of a hyperghettoized environment where more than 40 percent of residents live in poverty. William J. Wilson states:

> Since the 1970s, inner city neighborhoods have experienced an outmigration of working- and middle-class families previously confined to them by the restrictive covenants of higher-status city neighborhoods and suburbs. Combined with the increase in the number of poor caused by rising joblessness, this outmigration has sharply concentrated the poverty in inner-city neighborhoods. The number with poverty rates that exceed 40 percent—a threshold definition of "extreme poverty" neighborhoods—has risen precipitously. And the dwindling presence of middle- and working-class households has also removed an important social buffer that once deflected the full impact of the kind of prolonged high levels of joblessness in these neighborhoods that has stemmed from uneven economic growth and periodic recessions.[12]

This is what Grandmaster Flash and the Furious Five call the jungle. It is a part of the city where the middle class and upper class have abandoned their brothers and sisters who are locked in a cycle of poverty that has produced a permanent underclass. These people are locked in and locked out; bell hooks puts it this way:

> More and more, our nation is becoming class-segregated. The poor live with and among the poor—confined in gated communities without adequate shelter, food, or

health care—the victims of predatory greed. . . . No one safeguards the interests of citizens there; they are soon to be the victims of class genocide. This is the passive way our country confronts the poor and indigent, leaving them to die from street warfare, sugar, alcohol, and drug addiction, AIDS, and/or starvation.[13]

This is the truth of the matter. This is the truth of what "The Message" conveys, and the beat moves the hearer to understand. When you watch the video of "The Message," you see the world that Robin Kelley, William J. Wilson, and bell hooks write about. It is a world of pain and hurt that appears almost impossible to climb out of. This is the truth in the message, the truth of a lived experience that the listeners, the emcee, and the DJ can relate to. "The Message" becomes our story, as much as it is their story. Once again the truth is in the story, a story that reflects the truth. The truth is the redeeming quality in hip-hop.

Hip-hop as seen in "The Message" is the prophetic voice of hip-hop calling out. Like Jeremiah, hip-hop is crying out as it critiques and engages the plight of those it speaks for and to.

Hip-hop as seen in "The Message" is the prophetic voice of hip-hop calling out. Like Jeremiah, hip-hop is crying out as it critiques and engages the plight of those it speaks for and to. Hip-hop is looking at the political centers and religious leaders, critiquing them while crying out for help. The question is, will the leaders hear hip-hop? Will they listen to the cry? Will they come alongside hip-hop and help, or will they condemn the screaming voice from within?

Hip-hop is situated in the gray space, much like the prophet Jeremiah was. Jeremiah was in that gray space between hope and promise during a time when things appeared to get worse. This is what hip-hop has had to deal with. Hip-hop came on the scene after the civil rights movement, only to realize that civil rights didn't result in silver rights, a livable wage. The African American middle class had been elevated and had escaped the 'hood. The former prophets who had graced the pulpits of black churches had been gunned down or beaten down, and their prophetic message of social justice had been replaced by the prosperity gospel of Creflo Dollar and Fred Price. The prophetic message that had once been in the hands of the black church had been abandoned, and now hip-hop prophets had to pick up where the institutional church had left off. Todd Boyd put it best when he said, "Hip-hop has rejected and now replaced the pious, sanctimonious nature of civil rights as the defining moment of Blackness. In turn, it offers new ways of seeing and understanding what it means to be Black at this pivotal time in history."[14] It is the role of defining and understanding the life circumstances of what it means to be black—and especially black and working class—that positions hip-hop as a prophetic voice for the present age.

In the past, the black church served as a leader with others as they fought side by side for justice. Cornel West says, "The civil rights movement succeeded primarily because of the talent, skill, and courage of the civil rights activists, its pronounced black cultural potency (rooted in black southern churches), and the rising tide of political liberalism facilitated by an expanding American economy (at home and abroad)."[15] The very success of this movement, as attested to by West, also fueled the downfall of the center of the African American community. As the rising tide lifted the black church to the top, it took its money, status, and privilege and left the inner city; it ran to the suburbs. The African American church became a bastion for middle-class African Americans. As we look back over the past twenty years, the words of C. Eric Lincoln and Lawrence H. Mamiya sound prophetic. They suggested that the greatest challenge for the African American church in the twenty-first century was going to be reaching hardcore, inner-city, working-class African Americans; this was not the case for the African American church of the twentieth century. Lincoln and Mamiya state:

> The demographic movement of middle-income blacks out of inner city areas and into residential parts of the cities, older suburbs, or into newly created suburbs, has meant a growing physical and social isolation of the black poor. . . . The gradual emergence of two fairly distinct black Americas along class lines—of two nations within a nation—has raised a serious challenge to the Black Church. The membership of the seven historic black denominations is composed largely of middle-income working-class and middle-class members, with a scattering of support from poorer members, especially those in southern rural areas who tend to be among the most loyal members. But black pastors and churches have had a difficult time in attempting to reach the hard-core urban poor, the black underclass, which is continuing to grow. In past generations some of the large urban black churches were one of the few institutions that could reach beyond class boundaries and provide a semblance of unity in black communities. The challenge for the future is whether black clergy and their churches will attempt to transcend class boundaries and reach out to the poor, as these class lines continue to solidify with demographic changes in black communities. If the traditional Black Church fails in its attempts to include the urban poor, the possibility of a Black Church of the poor may emerge, consisting largely of independent, fundamentalist, and Pentecostal storefront churches. There also may emerge cults and sectarian forms of new religious movements among the black poor, similar to those exotic groups that emerged in the 1930s.[16]

The black church is now looking this reality square in the face. It is finding it difficult to reach inner-city, working-class, working-poor, and nonworking-poor African Americans. But the communities that are difficult for the African American church to reach are the very places hip-hop culture lives. It reaches out, touches, affirms, and communicates with the pain, struggles, and realities of these communities. The face of the black church has changed; its membership does not consist of many in the hip-hop generation. The sociological analysis and prophecy of Lincoln and Mamiya have come to pass. The class divide within the African American community is partially responsible for hip-hop being the first major cultural movement rooted in African American culture that wasn't nurtured by the African American institutionalized church. Hip-hop was nurtured by the very streets from which the African American church retreated and now finds difficult to reach. The institutionalized church didn't nurture and lead the hip-hop prophetic movement. As the class divide within the African American community widened, the black church continued to become a middle-class bastion.

The prophetic role of the church as a nurturer and leader championing a move for social change has been delegated to the hip-hop prophet who speaks from and to the social location of the inner-city working class. When Tupac came out with *2Pacalypse Now* in 1991, he essentially became a new Martin Luther King Jr. for pastors locked in middle-class African American churches who were incapable of crossing the class divide as did Martin Luther King Jr. and his peers. Tupac, along with his peers, became the prophet of the day. When Lorenz Tate, one of the leading voices and actors of the hip-hop generation, talked about Tupac, he spoke for a generation: "For most of his core fans and people who knew him, he was a prophet."[17] Or as Tupac's mother, Afeni Shakur, put it, "Artists are messengers from God. They get here on earth and express themselves because of Him."[18] In the hip-hop nation, artists were no longer just artists; they had morphed into something else. They had become leaders, preachers, prophets, and pastors for the generation that found itself outside the church.

The early 1990s serves as a marker for this break. During this time, Tupac came out with the previously mentioned *2Pacalypse Now*, and in March of 1992, the much-heralded group Arrested Development proclaimed that they were fishing for a new religion. Why were hip-hop and Arrested Development fishing for a new religion?[19] According to Arrested Development, the church was not making significant strides for positive change in the African American community or for the inner-city poor. The church was asking them to praise God and pray while not acting. The church was literally making them fall asleep. The church was ignoring what was happening in the 'hood. The church's inactivity was the exact opposite of what hip-hop was calling them to do. Hip-hop was bringing the life and struggles of the inner city to light. It was making a comment, critique, and response to the pain of inner-city living.

As those in hip-hop became social critics, they drew fans to the art form who weren't sympathetic about social change but rather saw it as a form of rebellion. This resulted in the emergence of the white, suburban hip-hop fan during this same period. Run-D.M.C. had invited whites and others to "Walk This Way," and the Beastie Boys had fought for their right to party. With hip-hop now on MTV and BET, the fan base wasn't all socially conscious or down with the cause.[20]

Furthermore, in hip-hop, the voice of activism and social critique emerges but with an absence of real activism. Bakari Kitwana says, "As activist minded as their lyrics may be, as tuned in as they are to activists' concerns, and as much as hip-hop generationers admire their politicized messages and activities, few are in the trenches day to day working to bring about change."[21] Kitwana is in essence saying that the hip-hop generation is activist minded but has yet to mobilize a true activist movement. One of the major reasons for this, according to Todd Boyd, is that the generation of leaders that led and nurtured the civil rights movement didn't nurture the next generation of leaders. Rather, they effectively alienated the next generation of potential leaders. Boyd, in his book *The New H.N.I.C.: The Death of Civil Rights and the Reign of Hip-Hop*, says, "Many in the civil rights era have for too long gloated in a sanctimonious fashion, assuming that their day would never come to an end. This arrogant posture did little to inspire a new generation but went a long way toward alienating them."[22] Not only did the civil rights leaders alienate the next generation, they also failed to integrate the next generation into their organizations. As a result, the civil rights organization became irrelevant and disconnected from hip-hop.

The civil rights leaders and the majority of church leaders acted in the same fashion with the same results. Hip-hop artists who have emerged as the voice of the future serve in the role of prophet to the culture and increasingly ask big questions without significant dialogue with their elders. This is not by choice but is a result of the rejection of hip-hop and hip-hop culture by the elders in the African American community. While the institutionalized church and other leaders of yesterday began to critique and stand against hip-hop, hip-hop embraced its theomusicological roots and continued to do—just as C. Eric Lincoln and Lawrence Mamiya said—what Tupac and Arrested Development told us was happening: they went fishing for a new religion, or at least a theology rooted in music.

Track 5: Hip-Hop and Its Continuation of African American Theomusicological History

Hip-hop didn't fall from the sky. Hip-hop is a child of African American culture. Its roots run deep. The civil rights elders may have cut hip-hop out of the leadership transition, but hip-hop couldn't be cut off from the cultural roots of African American musical history. Hip-hop continues the long legacy of African American art and artists that have served as prophets. Wyatt Tee Walker says, "The music, religion and culture of Black Americans are fundamentally African, both in form and substance."[23] Hip-hop is a child of the art that came before it; hip-hop is black art founded in the rich tradition of African and African American culture. Because hip-hop is a child of rhythm and blues, spirituals, and the blues, the child resembles and acts like the parents, being a political and prophetic voice for the people. James Cone, in his book *The Spirituals and the Blues*, says that "black music is political because in its rejection of white cultural values, it affirms the political 'otherness' of black people. Through song, a new political consciousness is continuously created, one antithetical to the values of white society. Black music is also theological. That is, it tells us about the divine Spirit that moves the people toward unity and determination."[24] Cone's characterization of the blues can also be applied to hip-hop, as hip-hop is also a rejection of white cultural values and it affirms the political significance of the lives of its listeners. We find in hip-hop culture a political value system and consciousness.

Hip-hop continues the long legacy of African American art and artists that have served as prophets.

One of the keys to understanding hip-hop is to see it as a culture with beliefs, values, and norms. Hip-hop culture then moves its listeners by framing the world, their world, as the other. The hip-hop artists understand their role as being what Patricia Hill Collins, social theorist and Distinguished University Professor of Sociology at the University of Maryland, describes as the "outsider within." As much as they are a part of mainstream dominant culture, as it promotes their music, they still speak from the margins. Their artists come from the margins. Hip-hop lyrics represent the sentiments and struggles of those on the margins of American society. This otherness represented in hip-hop culture takes on a political dynamic of resistance and survival. Hip-hop artists say, "We will survive despite the overt oppression and ghetto-class status that we and those we represent have been subjected to."

Though hip-hop has grown to become an international culture, its roots are in the African diasporic community. Moreover, as hip-hop travels around the globe, the artists and cultures that embrace hip-hop still look to African Americans as their icons, and they are compared to the founders of the culture when it comes to being authentically hip-hop.[25] Imani Perry argues that hip-hop is a creation of African American culture. She goes so far as to say, "Hip-hop music is black American music. Even with its hybridity: the consistent contributions from nonblack artists, and the borrowings from cultural forms of other communities, it is nevertheless black American music."[26] Perry doesn't deny the multicultural influences in hip-hop, but her analysis sees hip-hop as primarily lodged in the African American cultural context. While Perry uses what she calls an Afro-Atlantic theoretical frame for her analysis, I will use Afrocentricity as the theoretical frame by which to guide an analysis that will lead to an understanding and definition of hip-hop culture. If we look at hip-hop from a Eurocentric point of view, the analysis will produce a misunderstanding and ill-appropriation of hip-hop. As Molefi Kete Asante says:

> An analysis of African American culture that is not based on Afrocentric premises is bound to lead to incorrect conclusions. In a similar manner, the interpretation of

historical data from a strictly Eurocentric perspective can cause serious intercultural conflict, based on wrong premises.[27]

To understand hip-hop and its various strands around the globe, we must begin with the roots of hip-hop. An Afrocentric analysis of hip-hop ties it back to its African roots. Hip-hop has a history. Hip-hop evolved out of the rich cultural heritage of the African diaspora. Establishing this point will further contextualize hip-hop and help you see the natural sociocultural progression that hip-hop represents. To look at hip-hop as simply a late-twentieth-century development, isolated from its historical roots, misses the power, point, and progressive prophetic role of hip-hop as a child of African American culture. Looking at hip-hop involves looking back at Africa and looking around at how Africans were and are dispersed around the globe. The core of African diasporic culture continues to inform the development of conscious African American music and the totality of diasporic art and culture.

> *An Afrocentric analysis of hip-hop ties it back to its African roots. Hip-hop has a history.*

We can identify the direct link between hip-hop and African American culture in the use and power of language. The driving force beneath hip-hop culture is language, specifically as it mutates into the form of story with the power of the narrative. To help us understand the power of language as a tool that carries, maintains, sustains, and reconnects cultural roots, we call on Ngugi wa Thiong'o. Thiong'o, in his book *Decolonising the Mind*, posits the argument that language is a carrier of culture. He says, "Language, any language, has a dual character: it is both a means of communication and a carrier of culture. . . . Culture embodies those moral, ethical and aesthetic values, the set of spiritual eyeglasses, through which they come to view themselves and their place in the universe."[28] Language in hip-hop serves its first role as a means of communication. It is meant to tell us something. It carries the story over the beat. And embedded in the story are the moral and ethical values of hip-hop culture. There is also an aesthetic quality inherent in hip-hop in that the storyteller must have flavor, flow, rhyming skills, creativity, and a distinct character to his or her voice. As one engages the values embedded in the story via language, one then begins to see the set of spiritual eyeglasses that hip-hop offers those who want to understand hip-hop culture. The spiritual eyeglasses shared among the members of the hip-hop nation help one see how they view themselves and understand their place in the universe. It isn't for the listener to judge, correct, or fix but first to seek to understand.

It is important to remember, according to Thiong'o, that "values are the basis of a people's identity, their sense of particularity as members of the human race. All this is carried by language. Language as culture is the collective memory bank of a people's experience in history. Culture is almost indistinguishable from the language that makes possible its genesis, growth, banking, articulation and indeed its transmission from one generation to the next."[29] As one seeks to understand the values in hip-hop (values being those shared ideas about how things are ranked in terms of relative social desirability, worth, or goodness), this leads to an understanding of the things hip-hop promotes. Sociologically, values are the basis for norms (norms being expectations related to behavior). As language acts as a carrier of culture, it also promotes values and norms, which are rooted in the history of the culture or movement. Therefore, to study the history and cultural values of hip-hop, one has to be in touch with the ways language is used in hip-hop to construct the narrative that tells the history of the people and the art. To follow the transmission of hip-hop culture from its African roots down through the tree that is African American culture and art to the first-generation hip-hop artist and then to the second-generation hip-hop artist, one must look at the language that carries hip-hop culture.

Track 6: Unpacking the Story Structure of Hip-Hop

As we talk about hip-hop, let us never forget the breadth and depth of hip-hop culture. While hip-hop includes pervasive visual images, hip-hop culture rides on the language and story of hip-hop and in hip-hop. The world of hip-hop is created via a spoken word. In the beginning, God *said*, and it was so. The creative power of the word lies at the foundation of the Christian faith. Jesus spoke and something happened. Jesus spoke and Lazarus got up. In the world of hip-hop, the rapper speaks. His or her position as the emcee/storyteller is situated in one of three major frames. Tupac Shakur said, "I'm just trying to speak about things that affect me and about the things that affect our community. . . . Sometimes I'm the watcher, and sometimes I'm the participant, and sometimes it's just allegories or fables that have an underlying theme."[30] One frame or situation is that of the emcee as the watcher, one who speaks from what he or she has seen or retells a story with which he or she is familiar. In this position, the emcee serves as a reporter. In the role of participant, the emcee testifies to personal experiences in life. As the teller of a fable or allegory, the emcee takes a large story and uses it as a metaphor with an embedded truth that speaks to the values and norms of hip-hop. In the end, emcees are trying to speak truth. They are trying to speak truth about what they have seen or experienced, or they are trying to speak truth in the context of a larger story.

We will use Albert Murray's formula to tease out the truth in the drama that unfolds in hip-hop. Murray starts by describing the role of the story when he says, "A story is a work of the writer's imagination. It seldom follows an actual occurrence with the step-by-step accuracy of the historical record—and even when it does, each step immediately becomes an act in a play which the story-teller has contrived from the original events."[31] Hip-hop is based on true stories, some more true than others, but all true stories are still re-created by the story-teller. The storyteller—even in his or her desire to be as accurate as possible in regard to the actual events—is creating an act on a track or in a video. The stories in hip-hop are woven on top of beats, with images evoked by the powerful use of words that are carefully crafted by the storyteller to paint a picture in the minds and hearts of the listeners. Murray puts it this way:

> The story teller works with language, but even so, he is a song and dance man (a maker of *molpês*) whose fundamental objectives are extensions of those of the bard, the minstrel, and the ballad maker. . . . When he creates short stories and novels, the writer no less than these ancient Greek playwrights is composing and choreograph-ing song and dance situations of experience. It is by means of such imitations that he evokes the dynamic image which embodies and expresses his conception of human nature and of the meaning and purpose of human conduct.[32]

We can talk about the stories in hip-hop as comedy, tragedy, melodrama, or farce. According to Murray, the tragedy is an enactment of an encounter with death; the comedy in general deals with love; then there is the melodrama; and the farce revolves around subversion. These four story forms fit hip-hop well. Hip-hop deals with the deep issues of life, and no subject is off-limits. Hip-hop connects with those who are a part of the hip-hop nation as the storytellers bring their stories to life in the rap songs they experience. As Murray says, "When the writer relates a story to the reader, he literally *connects* him with what the story is about. He makes the reader aware of information which establishes a relationship between the reader and the writer's point of view, his scale of values, and his sense of human existence."[33]

When the emcee raps, listeners hear the rap in the form of a story. With each verse, the story unfolds, and the chorus leads listeners in and out of the verses. The best storytellers make the greatest connections—with the content of the story, with the way it is told or structured, and with the beat. The beat is also a part of the story. A beat that moves the story along facilitates the con-nection between the teller and the hearer. The track that the story rides on demands a nod, a nod to the beat, in connection with the truth in the story, to which listeners nod their heads in agreement. At some point along the way, the emcee's story becomes a shared story between the emcee and the hearers. The hearers are initiated into the ritual and making of the song; the song no longer belongs solely to the emcee. At some point it becomes their song, their story. So they repeat each word together as they feel the kick drum on the one and the three with the snares in between. The emcee and the hearers are now rhyming together, making story as they bounce to the beat.

The emcee as storyteller paints a picture of a hero in his or her work. Rap is about being an overcomer. Whether the main character in a song is defeating a fellow rapper in a rap battle or an enemy in a gun battle, winning the lover in a relationship battle, or overcoming poverty and oppression, rap goes back to the hero. The storyteller comes from the margins. Even if hip-hop artists have climbed the corporate ladder like a Jay-Z or Diddy, they still relate to where they came from, and despite arriving in the corner office, they still see their acceptance by the industry as by force. In the battle for acceptance, the art form and the culture of hip-hop have been tolerated by capitalist culture but not fully accepted. The market has used hip-hop as a moneymaker, but the dominant culture has not celebrated hip-hop as art. Hip-hop senses this strange relationship it has with America, and this outsider-within relationship fuels the depth and power of the art and the culture.[34] It moves artists to be serious and passionate writers, and their experience of rejection shapes and informs their story. According to Murray, "Serious writers have had a deep-seated sense of exclusion, disaffection, alienation, disillusionment, detachment, dissatisfaction, disorientation, and so on, and . . . this as much as anything is what makes them tick as writers."[35] When you experience hip-hop story as the lament that it is, then the power comes through.

> *The emcee as storyteller paints a picture of a hero in his or her work. Rap is about being an overcomer.*

The situation that produced serious writers in the past continues to birth serious writers now in the context of hip-hop. These writers share their deep-seated sense of exclusion as they stand apart from white America and middle-class black America. Their marginalization as writers, artists, and as a culture gives power, truth, and victory to their work. Despite being central in American culture, hip-hop is still an outsider within and has a strange position of being marginalized. To hear the truth in hip-hop, it is important to sit on the side of the road and listen within the context from which hip-hop comes.

The heroes in hip-hop overcome from the outside. They use their position as an outsider to attack the mainstream, to enter in the back door and take over. They slay the dragons of poverty, oppression, and abuse while learning to survive in the midst of them and at times leaving the pain of the 'hood for greener pastures. Hip-hop helps

> real-life and storybook heroes alike, not only by generating the necessity for heroism in the first place but by contesting its development at every stage and by furnishing the occasion for its fulfillment. Indeed, since in the final analysis the greatness of the hero can be measured only in scale with the mischief, malaise, or menace he can dispatch, the degree of cooperation is always equal to the amount of antagonism.[36]

The stories in hip-hop set the stage for the hero to emerge. He or she comes from the 'hood as a victim who will become a victor by track sixteen. To be victorious may mean to survive the 'hood or to slay those who oppose them. The stage is set on track one, and as you ride with the hero over the next fifteen tracks, there will be many twists and turns. In the end, however, survival as victory is the conquest worth the wait. Young Buck, like many artists, takes these journeys on his albums. Young Buck starts *Buck the World* with the track "Hold On" and ends with "Lose My Mind."[37] As we go on this journey, we see his twists and turns, victories and defeats, but in the end he is an overcoming survivor and a victor over the circumstances of pain, poverty, family tragedy, and industry battles. These are the battlegrounds and wars that hip-hop stories reveal as we follow the heroes.

Rap artists as heroes resonate with their listeners/followers. After all, these conquerors come from their ranks. These are average people, of average means, with average backgrounds who slay the dragons of oppression.

> The actual physical appearance of even the greatest heroes, for all their charisma, is frequently so unimposingly average that special effort seems necessary in order to set them apart from the proverbial man in the street. It is as if the typical hero has to be borne on the shoulders of worshipful admirers, bedecked with special raiments, elevated to special platforms, and thence to thrones and ultimately to pedestals in order that he may look impressive enough to be capable of the miraculous feats of championship which he has in fact already accomplished.[38]

As much as hip-hop artists boast, brag, and show off their bodies, they are bolstered by their supporters. In hip-hop, the artist is lifted up. This is done by his or her boasting and the followers' worship of the art and the artist. This isn't a culture of popularity or a contest of popularity, but it is one of conquest in that the hero is lifted up by the followers of hip-hop who give status to the artist. The power of the rhymes, the alienation of opposing camps via the rhymes, or the wordsmithing of the artist is what leads to his or her exaltation. The hero is looked at as having special gifts to slay others. It is the slaying of giants for which hip-hop is known. It is in hip-hop, via the beats and the rhymes, that one learns how to survive.

Track 7: The Blues in Hip-Hop from Moses to Joseph

Hip-hop is the Joseph story personified. Albert Murray laments that the African American community has embraced the exodus story and the Moses metaphor to the detriment of Joseph's story. The exodus has been emphasized as a departing or freedom anthem, but in reality African Americans haven't left America; they are still here.[39] So the question becomes, if African Americans aren't going anywhere, how do they survive in America? Hip-hop answers this question. Hip-hop moves from the Moses and exodus story to the Joseph story. Murray suggests that Moses focuses on going home and setting God's people free. In the Joseph story, we see a brother in captivity who finds a home in a foreign place. For Joseph, "home was as much a matter of the spirit as of real estate, anywhere he is can become the Land of Promise."[40] For hip-hop it can be the Dirty South, New York, the Midwest, the Third Coast (Houston), or the wild, wild West. They are all home to hip-hop. Hip-hop has gone global and has found a home. Hip-hop has made those places home and has found a way not only to survive but also to thrive. Hip-hop has transcended its outsider status much as Joseph, the "riff-style improviser, did to slavery. He transcended it to such an extent that his previous 'condition of servitude' became the sort of apocryphal cotton patch-to-capital detail so typical of U.S. biography."[41] This is hip-hop, from the streets to the Academy Awards (3-6 Mafia). Hip-hop has made a place in America for its story to be told and heard. In telling its story of struggle in America and surviving in the midst of this struggle, hip-hop artists have been empowered and have empowered others.

The telling of the story of pain as a way to treat that pain isn't new to hip-hop. Storytelling through song as a balm is rooted in African American culture and music. An example of this healing and empowerment story is found in the music of the blues. Because hip-hop is a child of the blues, we hear the blues in hip-hop. The blues told the truth about the experience of those trapped in poverty, and the telling of those stories was liberating. Larry Neal puts it this way: "Even though the blues may be about so-called hard times, people generally feel better after hearing them or seeing them. They tend to be ritually liberating in that sense."[42] Blues stories found a way into the souls of their hearers, and in hip-hop the story as healing continues, as the child of the blues grows up and becomes the griot. The telling of these stories, the hearing of these stories, and the healing of these stories become ritualistic for the hearers and the artists. "This is liturgy in which barefaced blues people came face-to-face with the truth of human existence, and the black experience, as preached to them in the blues, was a means of their discerning life's bare theological meaning."[43] As hip-hop comes face-to-face with the struggles of the hip-hop nation as told in its stories, it becomes liturgy. The tradition continues as hip-hop, like the blues, operates therapeutically in the life of the hip-hop nation.

Music in the African American tradition has served as a type of therapy for centuries. Jon Michael Spencer quotes Leonard Goines, who "argued that the music functioned for blacks in the same way professional therapy functioned

> *The power of the rhymes, the alienation of opposing camps via the rhymes, or the wordsmithing of the artist is what leads to his or her exaltation. The hero is looked at as having special gifts to slay others. It is the slaying of giants that hip-hop is known for. It is in hip-hop, via the beats and the rhymes, that one learns how to survive.*

for whites. 'The therapist is not there to propose solutions to problems but to ask questions so that the patient can clearly come to see and understand the nature of this problem. It is assumed that once a problem can be clearly and simply defined, solutions will follow. The blues functions in the same manner, as an analysis of the lyrics clearly demonstrates.'"[44] Just as the blues served as a type of therapy, so does hip-hop. Hip-hop clearly and simply defines what is going on in the lives of those in the hip-hop nation. It describes their struggles and pains. It demystifies the inner city and its harsh living conditions. Hip-hop asks questions that lead those of the hip-hop nation to their communal and individual solutions. Hip-hop helps the nation understand the nature of the problems it faces in its world. So Ice Cube asks the question, "You wonder why in the f— we thugs?" on his album *Laugh Now, Cry Later*. He is essentially raising the question and then walking with his listeners as they think about the relationship between poverty, pain, and governmental suppression of their efforts for liberation. Hip-hop acts as therapy in this context.

The blues people, like the hip-hop nation, sought an answer to their plight via popular culture mixed with a version of the faith they had heard of, participated in, or bumped into by way of black religious institutions. Hip-hop, like the blues, is about survival.

Hip-hop preaches in ways similar to the way the black church preached for years. Hip-hop provides answers to the quandaries in life that the church has failed to address in ways acceptable to hip-hop. James Cone says, "Not all blacks could accept the divine promises of the Bible as satisfactory answers to the contradictions of black existence."[45] The blues people, like the hip-hop nation, sought an answer to their plight via popular culture mixed with a version of the faith they had heard of, participated in, or bumped into by way of black religious institutions. Hip-hop, like the blues, is about survival. As Cone says, black music "is not an artistic creation for its own sake; rather it tells us about the *feeling* and *thinking* of an African people, and the kinds of mental adjustments they had to make in order to survive in an alien land."[46] Hip-hop is about making adjustments to survive. The stories in hip-hop tell us strategies for survival as the griot shares the feelings and thoughts of the people of hip-hop.

As hip-hop artists tell of the means and tools of survival, their stories, laced with theology and religion, become secular spirituals. Cone says, "The blues are 'secular spirituals.' They are *secular* in the sense that they confine their attention solely to the immediate and affirm the bodily expression of black soul, including its sexual manifestations. They are *spirituals* because they are impelled by the same search for the truth of black experience."[47] In similar ways, hip-hop represents secular spirituals. The choruses and verses of rap lyrics address the bodily expression and existence of those who are members of the hip-hop nation. The sexual manifestations, fantasies, and contradictions are exposed in hip-hop in raw terms. The exposing of the bodily urges and struggles is linked directly to hip-hop's search for the truth of black experience, as well as the experience of others who are a part of the hip-hop nation. Joan Morgan says, "Truth is what happens when your cumulative voices fill in the breaks, provide the remixes, and rework the chorus."[48] Truth is found in this secular-spiritual quest as reality and fantasy meet; at that intersection, the remix produces the truth out of which rap via the hip-hop nation becomes that secular spiritual. To put it another way, hip-hop songs, like the blues, "are true because they combine art and life, poetry and experience, the symbolic and the real. They are an artistic response to the chaos in life."[49] It is this relationship between art and life, poetry and experience, the symbolic and the real that produces the truth in hip-hop as they are mixed and remixed.

As we look at the continuing legacy of the blues, we see how the blues and hip-hop function in similar ways. Hip-hop shares four primary characteristics with the blues:

1. Hip-hop *affirms the somebodiness* of the hip-hop nation.
2. Hip-hop *preserves the worth* of the hip-hop nation through ritual and drama.
3. Hip-hop *transforms the life* of hip-hoppas by rapping and singing about the life and struggles of the hip-hop nation.
4. Hip-hop symbolizes the solidarity, the attitudes, and the identity of the hip-hop nation and thus *creates the emotional forms of reference for endurance and aesthetic appreciation.*[50]

These four characteristics, which existed in the blues and now exist in hip-hop, affirm the "dictum: Truth is experience, and experience is the Truth. If it is lived and encountered, then it is real. There is no attempt in the blues to make philosophical distinctions between the divine and human truth."[51] As hip-hop affirms the somebodiness of the hip-hop nation, it makes an experiential claim that via this experience the hip-hop nation is somebody—a somebody who is heard and deserves to be heard. Hip-hop preserves the worth of the hip-hop nation by recording and retelling its story. This produces a transformative truth, for the experience isn't one of judgment but rather of journey. The journey of hip-hop symbolizes a shared solidarity. It is shared in the story that is a product of the truth of a lived experience. Hip-hop is concrete in its linking of story, truth, and experience, just like the blues. "The blues are not abstract; they are concrete. They are intense and direct responses to the reality of black experience."[52] Like the blues, hip-hop was born out of and was a direct response to the reality of the black experience, a working-class experience. Hip-hop frames the story out of which truth and experience are expressed and rehearsed. Like the blues, hip-hop gives structure to the experience that others try to articulate. "The purpose of the blues is to give structure to black existence in a context where color means rejection and humiliation."[53] As hip-hop stood outside the mainstream of African American culture and the music industry, artists expressed this pain of being outside, left out, and oppressed.

Hip-hop must be contextualized again and again. Many misunderstood or simply failed to understand the blues, and so many fail to understand hip-hop. "It is impossible to sing the blues or listen to their authentic presentation without recognizing that they belong to a particular community. They were created in the midst of the black struggle for being. And because the blues are an expression of that struggle, they are inseparable from blackness and trouble."[54] Hip-hop came out of the struggle of the late 1970s and the 1980s, during the birth of the Reagan era. Just as "the blues are the songs of men and women who have been hurt and disappointed and who feel the confusion and isolation of human love,"[55] so are the songs of hip-hop. The hip-hop generation is a hurting generation; all the promises from civil rights to hip-hop got lost in the mix-up, not the remix. The hopes of tomorrow became hope lost. We find in hip-hop an honesty about this loss.

Hip-hop came out of the struggle of the late 1970s and the 1980s, during the birth of the Reagan era. Just as "the blues are the songs of men and women who have been hurt and disappointed and who feel the confusion and isolation of human love," so are the songs of hip-hop.

Hip-hop, like the blues, is an honest music: "The blues are honest music. They describe every aspect of a woman's feelings about a man, and what a man thinks about a woman. Through the blues, black people express their views about infidelity and sex."[56] Critics of hip-hop—and hip-hop has a lot of room for critique—sometimes miss the honesty. Just the other day I had an exchange with a colleague about the misogyny, violence, and sexism in rap lyrics. She was complaining about the hate a young man was spewing out as he repeated the lyrics to a song on his iPod. She was angered by his words and wanted to confront him. Her question to me was, "What is honest or good about that?" My response to these valid critiques is rooted in what Joan Morgan says: it tells us how these young men feel. It tells us something about the state of male/female relationships. It tells us something about the pain and the chasm that has evolved in the hip-hop community as sexism has run rampant. To quote Morgan:

> As a black woman and a feminist I listen to the music with a willingness to see past the machismo in order to be clear about what I'm *really* dealing with. What I hear frightens me. . . . The seemingly impenetrable wall of sexism in rap music is really the complex

mask African Americans often wear both to hide and express the pain. At the close of the millennium, hip-hop is still one of the few forums in which young black men, even surreptitiously, are allowed to express their pain. . . . It's extremely telling that men who can only see us as "bitches" and "hos" refer to themselves only as "niggas."[57]

The truth in the misogyny, sexism, and violence in rap lyrics and hip-hop culture is that the young men are conflicted. This truth points to an experience that needs to be explored. It tells us what we are really dealing with. While men may pay lip service to the "Black Queen," on cut fourteen they are calling her a bitch or a ho. This then raises the question of tension and conflictedness. And as Morgan says, these men also refer to themselves as niggas. This points to the truth of the matter: there is a problem here that needs attention. Dialogue needs to be instituted that leads to repentance and actions that heal the brokenness in these relationships. Black men need to truly respect and fall in love with black women again. As much as some may be bothered by the sexism and misogyny, we have to listen if we want to hear the truth of what followers of hip-hop feel.

Morgan pushes us to ask why we listen and why we have to listen to hip-hop. The church and Christian institutions should think twice before turning a deaf ear to hip-hop and hip-hop culture. Hip-hop's lucid descriptions of sex and sexuality let us into a world that few in the church have explored or will admit to knowing. The sexuality as expressed in hip-hop tells the church something about how the hip-hop generation views love and loving relationships. I was surprised recently by a song by Akon. In the edited version of the song, Akon cries, "I want to love you," but in the unedited version of that same song, he sings, "I want to f— you." My question after listening to the two versions was, does this brother see f—ing and loving as synonymous? I am troubled by the descriptions of relationships and sex in hip-hop, but they allow me to see and hear what I would never know as a forty-five-year-old Christian man married to the same woman for twenty-five years.

James Cone says of the blues:

> It has been the vivid description of sex that caused many church people to reject the blues as vulgar or dirty. The Christian tradition has always been ambiguous about sexual intercourse, holding it to be divinely ordained yet the paradigm of rebellious passion. Perhaps this accounts for the absence of sex in the black spirituals and other church music. . . . In the blues there is an open acceptance of sexual love.[58]

Hip-hop, like the blues, includes open, frank discussions about sex and love. This honesty or openness tends not to exist in most churches or Christian institutions. Kelly Brown Douglas has made this argument well in her works on the black church, especially her book *The Black Church and Sexuality: Why the Black Church Can't Talk about Sex*. Douglas chides the church in her work, saying that if the church doesn't talk about sex, hip-hop becomes sex education

101 for those who listen, and the church needs to get involved in the conversation. Hip-hop invites the church to be involved in the dialogue if it so chooses.

As vile, vulgar, and violent as hip-hop can be, it deserves an ear from the church. Hip-hop speaks from the margins; it tells of a war zone. Joan Morgan says, "Black folks in nineties America are living and trying to love in a war zone. . . . Though it's often portrayed as a part of the problem, rap music is essential to that struggle because it takes us straight to the battlefield."[59] Hip-hop as embraced by blacks, whites, yellows, and browns connects people for different reasons, but the common denominator is the truth in hip-hop that calls them. The tales of pain, struggle, and survival in hip-hop mirror the world of the blues that told the truth about the survival strategies of blacks who had to deal with the contradictions of society. James Cone says, "The blues are lived experience, an encounter with the contradictions of American society but a refusal to be conquered by it. They are despair only in the sense that there is no attempt to cover up reality. The blues recognize that black people have been hurt and scared by the brutalities of white society."[60] Hip-hop testifies to the struggle of African Americans and others who are a part of the hip-hop nation. It exposes the emptiness in riches. As much as hip-hop glorifies the materialism of American culture, it also exposes the myth. As hip-hop struggles for meaning and purpose and continues its spiritual and religious quest, the question becomes, how do the church and Christian institutions engage hip-hop?

For the most part, hip-hop, like the blues, has chosen to live its spiritual and religious life outside the church. Robin Sylvan sums up the present-day religious landscape as it relates to hip-hop when he says, "The religious impulse has simply migrated to another sector of the culture, a sector in which religious sensibilities have flourished and made an enormous impact on a large portion of the population."[61] Hip-hop artists have taken religious discourse outside the walls of the institutionalized church much like blues singers did years ago, articulating their religious worldview in their lyrics and lifestyle. "Those who lived the life of the blues 'behind the mule' were a 'folk' people who tended to articulate their religious world outlook in lore and lyric rather than in scholarly discourse. As a result, blues scholars who had not immersed themselves in the whole of discourse about black culture were unable to recognize that the blues was authentically theological."[62] As James Cone suggests, the acts of hearing, feeling, and understanding the theology and religious worldview of hip-hop call for an immersion in the culture. The theological world of hip-hop is in between the verses and the chorus. It is laced over pounding beats. Hip-hop followers. are following their religious urges as they seek God in the age of hip-hop revolution. George Barna has reported that people aren't looking for a church but rather are trying to find out how to be church. It was ironic to me that, in the movie *Idlewild*, Outkast labeled the club "The Church." Their going to church was going to the club, and it was in the club that they found themselves and their purpose and had a divine meeting with God.

Hip-hop, like the blues, sees itself outside institutionalized religion (the church). As a result of being outside the church and apart from this formally recognized body, hip-hop critiques what it identifies as the church's hypocrisy. In similar ways, "Blues singers, true to their concise realism and directness, posited a myriad of observations about church folks' hypocrisy and self-righteousness and did so in a variety of moods ranging from the comic to the sardonic to the dogmatic."[63] We see this in Lyfe Jennings's song "Made Up My Mind," in which he calls the church a bunch of hypocrites. Will Smith also points to the hypocrisy of the church in his song "Ms. Holy Roller." And then there is T.I. He not only calls out organized religion but he also says that instead of fighting inner-city youth and young adults and putting them in jail the institutional church should be praying for them. He confesses they need help.

Like the blues singers before them, the hip-hop community is crying out, but because they feel like outcasts from the church, they cry out in the streets. These modern-day laments are loud and clear if we care to listen. Do we hear? In the 1920s, Thomas Dorsey heard God through the blues. Dorsey was able to make a marriage between the blues and the gospel. The church fought the move, but eventually what we now know as gospel music merged the blues' musical sensibilities with truth. The challenge today is whether the church will hear hip-hop the way it eventually heard the blues.

The chasm is wide between the institutionalized church and hip-hop, but it can be bridged. The first step in this bridge is for the church to listen to hip-hop and study hip-hop culture. Immerse yourself in the history of hip-hop and help shape its future.

Getting in Touch with Hip-Hop

Grandmaster Flash and the Furious Five. *The Message*. Sugar Hill, 1982.
Hamilton, Anthony. *Ain't Nobody Worryin'*. So So Def, 2005.
2Pac. *2Pacalypse Now*. Jive, 1991.

4

i used to love her
and i still love her

Loving the Broken Beauty of Hip-Hop

Common Sense of Common: Whose Side Are You On?

The year is 1994 and Common Sense hasn't yet become Common. He would morph into Common in 1997, and by 2007 he would have a number one record on the Billboard charts. His album *Finding Forever* wouldn't be his first charting album—there was *Be* before *Finding Forever*.[1] On his 1994 song "I Used to Love Her," Common Sense critiques hip-hop for selling out and becoming, as he put it, "gimmicky." Common Sense was also critical of hip-hop's appeal to the suburbs, interest in money, talk of violence, and degradation of women.[2] Common Sense seemed to make sense. But did Common become what Common Sense complained about in 1994?

Those of us who enjoy hip-hop can be caught in this conflicted state. We appear to have two sides. On one side there is a hip-hop fan, and on the other side there is a hip-hop critic. This chapter suggests that these are two sides of the same coin. We can embrace and even love hip-hop while being critical of the very thing we love or enjoy. It is out of our love for hip-hop that our loving critique is born.

MCA/Photofest

Common: a voice of consciousness from the Midwest

Track 1: I Ain't on No Side: I Am Hip-Hop

When people talk to me, a preacher and a professor in his mid-forties, and find out that I teach theology and hip-hop culture, they don't know how to respond. They think the two just don't go together. The most interesting response comes from my generational peers and Christians who don't know what to make of me and my connection to hip-hop. The conversation is usually a bit tense and guarded at first, but I always brace myself for the ultimate question: "So what do you think about hip-hop?" In most cases, they are on the side of the critic and want me either to yell out with them, "Stone hip-hop," or defend hip-hop. I respond by telling my story and how I came to hip-hop. I can't say I am hip-hop in the truest sense, but like Jon Michael Spencer said about his connection to the blues, "Though I do not feel I can say 'I am the blues,' I can say comfortably that I 'belong to' the blues, part and parcel, because I know what it means to be black and currently living on the underside of history."[3] I am not hip-hop, but I sure belong to hip-hop.

But how is this possible? Listen to Houston Baker:

> How then does the Black Studies scholar "inside" the academy productively sound the territories of rap and analyze its "outside" energies in meaningful ways? First, one has to attempt stylistically and historically to move in harmony with the form's own displacements. Next, I believe, one needs to theorize the form's resonances in terms of—to quote KRS-One—"Where you are and what you do." "Inside" and "outside" might thus converge in strategic forms of instructional resistance for the future.[4]

I belong to hip-hop as a scholar in his mid-forties who is on the margins of hip-hop but is also called to use his position as an outsider within the academy to write about hip-hop. I can't rap, but I can write, and my writing is a part of the remix.

68 ———— chapter 4

When I publicly declare that I am a professor and a preacher who teaches and writes about hip-hop, I go on to say that I love hip-hop; I have been grafted into the family. For better or worse, hip-hop and I have been wedded. In most cases, those whom I engage in conversation are amazed if not shocked when I say, "I love hip-hop. I actually enjoy the culture." My conversation partners then tell me how they feel about hip-hop. I haven't met a person who held back. They let me have it. The blame-it-on-hip-hop litany follows. I can't count the number of times people have said, "Well, you know, if it wasn't for hip-hop we wouldn't have _____ [fill in the blank]." I call this the blame-it-on-hip-hop line; everybody seems to have one. Inevitably, I hear, "How do you deal with the sexism, misogyny, and violence in hip-hop?" I pause and begin a patient but calculated answer. As the conversation progresses, I am asked, "So where is hip-hop going and what do you make of it?" I invoke Mos Def, verbatim. In response to the question of how hip-hop is doing, Mos Def says on the track "Fear Not of Man" that what is going to happen to hip-hop is going to happen to us; in essence, he says we are hip-hop. If hip-hop goes left, we go left; if hip-hop goes right, we go right. We are hip-hop. Hip-hop isn't off somewhere in a remote village. It is in us.[5]

Those of you who care enough to read this book, listen to hip-hop, and embrace some part of hip-hop culture are hip-hop in some way. Be you black, white, red, brown, or yellow, you are in some way hip-hop. So as we engage in a critique of hip-hop, we have to start by looking in the mirror. Too many of my conversation partners want to talk about hip-hop as if it were, as Mos Def would say, "a giant livin' in the hillside." Hip-hop isn't a giant living in the hillside coming down to visit the townspeople. Hip-hop isn't the boogeyman. Hip-hop is us, and we are hip-hop. We as members of the hip-hop nation have a say on where hip-hop is going and what it becomes.

If we are hip-hop in some form or fashion, how can we be against ourselves? How can we be divided and conflicted? How can we embrace something and be critical of it at the same time? There are some things about ourselves that we love, and then there are other things about ourselves that we would like to change. The fact that a part of us isn't that great doesn't define the entirety of our being. For instance, I am a proud African American even though there are things in the past and present state of American affairs that I detest; I am still an African American. The things about America that I hate don't get in the way of the things about America that I love.

Just as I am an African American, I am a member of the hip-hop family. We shouldn't be forced to pick sides when it comes to hip-hop. Are you for hip-hop or against it? Are you for America or against it? We have to be more specific. As much as I am an African American, I am critical of the nation that I love. As much as I am of hip-hop, I am critical of the culture that I love. To be a part of something and be critical of it demands a complex set of lenses that allows us to move beyond tunnel vision. I find in my conversations about hip-hop that the critics I encounter for the most part suffer from tunnel vision. They focus on the worst in hip-hop. They have allowed hip-hop's bad moments to define their view. In most cases, they haven't taken the time to develop a hip-hop aesthetic or to look at hip-hop objectively to see both the good and the bad. They haven't allowed themselves to see how good hip-hop culture is and how good it makes you feel. I am a big Kanye West fan, and when I hear, "What don't kill me can only make me stronger," I feel good!

Track 2: It Feels Good: Developing a Hip-Hop Aesthetic

In hip-hop culture, as in all cultures, language carries the culture. Language names the culture and defines the culture. In hip-hop culture, the work of the emcee is central. If we are going to critique hip-hop culture, we need to develop a working aesthetic of hip-hop that focuses on the art of the culture, and that includes the emcee. An aesthetic of hip-hop culture provides us with a complete set of lenses to study, love, enjoy, and critique hip-hop culture.

William Jelani Cobb, in his book *To the Break of Dawn: A Freestyle on the Hip-Hop Aesthetic*, says that "to understand hip-hop as an *aesthetic*" means "to deal . . . with the art on its own terms."[6] To deal with hip-hop as an aesthetic, we must deal with the themes that are dealt with in hip-hop. To extend Cobb's aesthetic definition, I would add that artistic form and expression in hip-hop are central to developing an aesthetic of hip-hop culture. We can't talk about lyrical content without talking about the delivery of a rhyme. We can't talk about the delivery of a rhyme without taking into consideration the swagger, dress, attitude, and life history of the artist. A hip-hop aesthetic is crucial because it is through the aesthetic frame that one can appreciate the artistry of hip-hop culture while also not glossing over the content of the culture.

In his book *There's a God on the Mic: The True 50 Greatest MCs*, Kool Moe Dee outlines eighteen elements of an emcee:[7]

1. originality	7. flow	13. poetic value
2. substance	8. live	14. longevity
3. vocal presence	9. performance	15. vocabulary
4. industry impact	10. social impact	16. freestyle
5. battle skills	11. versatility	17. body of work
6. concepts	12. flavor	18. lyrics

Kool Moe Dee gives us a good start as we begin to think about a hip-hop aesthetic. To appreciate the work of an emcee, it is not enough to look at his or her greatest hit or to limit him or her to a region or hip-hop era (old skool, golden age, new skool). The eighteen elements, as defined by Kool Moe Dee, provide criteria that can be laid over the entire body of work of an emcee. Is the emcee original or simply a copycat? What does the emcee bring to the culture? What is his or her impact in the industry? Does the artistic production of the emcee make a social impact? If so, what type of impact? How does the artist lay down rhymes and define hip-hop culture? Is the emcee versatile in his or her style? Is his or her vocabulary diverse? Does the artist have a strong vocal presence? Can the emcee flow? What is the artist's body of work? Where has the emcee been, where is he or she taking the culture, how is the emcee defining hip-hop culture? Kool Moe Dee gives us an aesthetic lens to start with, and then he applies it to fifty emcees.

The aesthetic frame is built on the foundation of flow. Flow is the key element and foundation in the artistic production of hip-hop culture. Flow, as defined by Cobb, "is an individual time signature, that rapper's own idiosyncratic approach to the use of time. Flow has two basic characteristics: the division of syllables and the velocity at which they are spoken."[8] When we engage hip-hop culture as it comes through the speakers of our sound system, we need to listen to the flow of the emcee. What is his or her time signature? How is he or she chopping lyrics up to make them fit in that mathematical formula of four beats? As you nod your head to the beat of the words that define and create culture, how does the emcee pour out those very words we repeat?

> Flow is the Rosetta stone of lyrical understanding. Since there is seldom the same number of syllables or words from one line to the next, the rapper doesn't *speak* at the same speed from one line to the next. This is lyrical long division. Rapping through a standard sixteen-bar combination, the MC has to manage an equal number of changes in pitch, inflection, and delivery—all while maintaining breath control. The craft comes down to this: the trickiness of enunciation, the constant variation of speed, the tongue-twisting elongation or contraction of words. The MC is the mathematician.[9]

An aesthetic of hip-hop centers on how emcees do lyrical long division, how they chop up their words, how they make an idea, concept, or story fit in the formula of four, eight, or sixteen bars. What an emcee says is important, but the flow is equally important as an aesthetic criterion. How creative is the emcee while doing lyrical long division? How clever is the emcee with words? How does the emcee use pitch and inflection while maintaining breath control? How does the emcee use silence? These are aesthetic questions that push us to see the art in the culture.

The emcee uses words to create the culture, just as in the beginning God created the heavens and the earth by speaking them into existence (Gen. 1:1–3). But the emcee creates over a beat that can't be dismissed. The beat is a part of the aesthetic frame. When the beat is dope or hot, our heads begin to move up and down. The beat serves the purpose of getting the hearer to say, "Yes, I am open to the rhyme." The fact that the head is moving up and down, saying yes, is evidence of how important the beat is as a creative artistic partner in the culture. The beat, or the track, exposes us to the creative synergy between emcee and beat maker. The beat can't be ignored or fully explained or understood. The track is a part of the aesthetic.

The partnership between emcee and DJ is key to some of the best hip-hop. In the next chapter, we look at the story of hip-hop as told by DMX. A key to DMX's success is his partnership with the DJ Swizz Beatz. The track must be analyzed and appreciated. How has the DJ mixed and remixed, sampled, taken liberty by doubling up the kick drum? How has he or she used the snares and synthesizers on the track? I try to tune out the lyrics and focus on the track as a way of getting at what the rhyme is riding on. I then reverse the process and focus almost exclusively on the rhyme. Finally, I put the two together, and my appreciation of both is increased. More importantly, this practice empowers me to see how the two work together, the beauty in the art of both as two parts of the one.

> *The beat serves the purpose of getting the hearer to say, "Yes, I am open to the rhyme."*

The track is what the rhyme rides on, but in many cases the rhyme is what is loudest, and it is often repeated. As we continue to tease out a hip-hop aesthetic, we have to move to listening to the power in the story of the rhyme. How well written is the story? While flow focuses on the delivery, analysis of the story asks a different set of questions:

What is the emcee saying?
What is the story?
Is it a quality (well-written, interesting, intriguing, gripping) story?
What are the plot elements?
Who are the characters?
What is the point of the story?
Do you buy into the story?
Can you follow the story?
Do you enjoy the hook in the story that repeats between the verses?
Does the hook amplify the story and serve to connect the verses?
Who are the good people and the bad people in the story?
Is it a story about good and evil?
What is the moral in the story?
What are the truth claims in the story?
Is the story based on a true story?
What category does the story fit into?
Is it a mystery?
Is it a testimony?

At least ten types of story formats typically show up on hip-hop albums. These ten formats can be broadly categorized as follows:

1. Prayers: In these songs, the artist overtly and directly prays.
2. Testimonials: These songs tell the life struggle and journey of the artist, which is confirmed by other sources.
3. Demonic dealings: These songs deal with the devil or evil forces.
4. Clique songs: Clique songs celebrate and call for community. I want to put them in the religious category, but they don't fit squarely. The call can be for those who run with or support the artist or those the artist ran with in the past.
5. Big question songs: Big question songs ask the major philosophical religious questions that are typically answered by religious traditions.
6. Bragging/party songs: The intent of bragging/party songs is to embellish or exaggerate the role of the artist. They are in the boasting tradition of African American culture and specifically hip-hop culture.
7. Crime glamour songs: These songs lift up or exalt criminal activity. When listening to these songs, hearers must place them in the context of the inner city, which is a war zone created for the poor. These songs also glamorize violence in the inner city as a way to sell the pain of poverty to middle-class America.
8. Love songs: These songs explore male-female relationships in hip-hop. They share how the hip-hop generation understands and experiences love and sex.
9. Statement songs: These are political songs or stories that take a political or revolutionary stance.
10. Dance/club bangers: These songs are made to be played in clubs for the specific purpose of making people dance.

Here are some questions to ask of the emcee in relation to the song:

Is the emcee a participant in the story?
Is the emcee telling a fable or an allegory?
Is the emcee the watcher?
Is the emcee just having fun?
Is the emcee using parody?
Is the emcee good at what he or she is trying to do?

These types of questions begin to lead us in the direction of an aesthetic for looking at the art that produces the culture. If we start with an aesthetic frame to help us appreciate and understand the art of hip-hop culture, we can then move to a posture of more critical engagement without missing the artistic value and contribution of the culture. A hip-hop aesthetic allows us to enjoy the artistic form while at the same time critiquing the content. To critique the content without respecting the artistic form is problematic; it invalidates the critique because the critic speaks from the outside.

Some of the biggest public critics of hip-hop haven't taken the time to appreciate the artistic value of hip-hop culture. I think about the debates that are led by people like Oprah Winfrey, Bill Cosby, Rev. Dr. Calvin Butts, Rev. Dr. Delman Coates, and Stanley Crouch. When you hear their critiques, you can tell they haven't listened to the story in hip-hop culture or taken the time to appreciate the artistic value of hip-hop culture. They haven't taken the time to hear the story or appreciate the way the story is being told. They haven't taken the time to consider the flow, content, or contextual placement of the story. To be redundant, the culture and truth are in the story.

When people come up to me and say, "How can you listen to hip-hop? It is so _____ [fill in the blank]," the first thing I ask them is, "What is the story of the song?" I don't want to hear what Bill O'Reilly said the song said. Did you listen to the song? Is the emcee you are talking about a good storyteller? Is the artist creative? Have you listened to the breadth of his or her work, or are you talking about one or two songs on the album? Have you listened to the entire album and begun to understand, appreciate, and contextualize his or her work? If you haven't done these things, it is going to be difficult for us to have an intelligent conversation about hip-hop culture. Many people want to critique hip-hop, but I find very few people who can critique hip-hop intelligently as a result of taking hip-hop seriously.

Track 3: Listening to the Dirty without Being Dirty: The Fanatic Critic

Being in my mid-forties and a hip-hop fan is a bit strange. This comes to light more than ever when I am riding in my midlife sports car with hip-hop banging through my Bose sound system, subwoofer rattling the mirrors, and my head moving up and down like a bobblehead doll. People pull up beside me and take two looks. I feel most embarrassed when I am reciting lyrics to a song that is filled with racy language (cursing or references to sex and certain body parts of females or males). I feel like there is something wrong with my moment of enjoyment. Here I am enjoying a song that is sexist, misogynistic, and vulgar. What is wrong with this picture? It is a picture that I find myself in quite often, as I listen to hip-hop constantly. I listen to hip-hop first because I like it and second because it is something I study. To be a fan and a student of hip-hop means that I listen to all of hip-hop. I listen to the good, the bad, and the vulgar. I listen to some edited but mostly unedited versions of hip-hop. The cursing means something, and it is a part of the verbal witness of hip-hop and the defining of the culture. Picking and choosing out of hip-hop culture is not something that a student has the privilege of doing. A student of hip-hop must try to be conversant with the culture at every level. If I am honest, some of the worst of the culture is something I am drawn to and at times actually enjoy.

Since I am in a confessional moment, I will say that one of my favorite songs of Tupac's is "Thug Passion." If you don't know this song, let me say that it is risqué to say the least. The song in its unedited version includes every curse word that good Christians shouldn't say. On most days I skip over the "bad" words by not saying them as I rap along. There are other days when I am so into the song that the words just seem to roll off my lips or repeat silently in my head. When I reflect on these moments, I ask, can this be good? I feel so guilty when I think about what I said as I enjoyed the song. When I am saying the words, I can't be thinking, can I? Maybe I am thinking about the song and trying to feel all of the song. Maybe for that five minutes and seven seconds, I am trying to totally feel what Tupac wrote. Maybe I am not thinking and simply enjoying the song as it was intended to be enjoyed. I can't have on my feminist ears as I listen because I am actually saying and thinking sexist thoughts. I can't have on my Methodist ears because this can't be moving me toward perfection. Maybe I have on my nonjudgmental hip-hop ears. Well, even those ears, my hip-hop ears, make judgments. I know this because as a fan I skip the songs I don't like when I am listening for fun. So what is going on in me and with me as I listen to songs like "Thug Passion"? I say "like" "Thug Passion" because there are many more I listen to that are worse or at least in the same vein.

I think about the debates that are led by people like Oprah Winfrey, Bill Cosby, Rev. Dr. Calvin Butts, Rev. Dr. Delman Coates, and Stanley Crouch. When you hear their critiques, you can tell they haven't listened to the story in hip-hop culture or taken the time to appreciate the artistic value of hip-hop culture.

I find myself caught in this quandary. What is going on here? How do we develop a model to be a part of hip-hop and not feel dirty? I don't know if I have an answer to this question. My tentative answer is that there are some parts of hip-hop culture that I don't feel I can come away from and not feel dirty. Just as I am proud to be a Christian, there are some parts of the church and things we do and endorse that leave me sick to my stomach, but I am still a Christian and an active member of the church. I have problems with war and even the just war theory, but I am still a proud Christian and American. When I see some of the things my country has done, I feel horrible, but I still love America. This is how I feel about hip-hop; I cannot reject hip-hop because some of the culture is base, raw, vulgar, dirty, misogynistic, sexist, materialistic, and downright degrading.

While I can appreciate the art form and celebrate it, at times I am offended by the very culture I am a part of. When I catch myself and come to myself, I critique the content of the culture that goes against my values and evolving moral code. I openly and vehemently must stand up and say, "Now _____ went too far on this one. I can't believe _____ said _____." I am not afraid to critique products of the culture that are incongruent with my value system or the values of my faith. While critiquing hip-hop, I don't dismiss it or not listen to what I critique, because I feel I can still learn something from it, even those most vulgar parts of the culture. Therefore, my critique is rooted in love and being honest about my own sexist tendencies. The critique of hip-hop culture is also a critique of myself and my relationship with the culture. I embrace this critique as not being incongruent with my love of the art and the story. I would say they are a part of my love affair with hip-hop. What I have concluded is that as much as I can be repulsed by parts of hip-hop culture, I can still learn from the culture.

Track 4: Suicidal Thoughts: Being Perplexed While in the Moment

Learning from the most vulgar parts of the culture is something I have struggled with from the beginning of my listening to hip-hop. Then I came across Joan Morgan's classic text, *When Chickenheads Come Home to Roost: My Life as a Hip-Hop Feminist*. As I was struggling with my decision to be exposed to the good, the bad, and the vulgar in hip-hop, Morgan came to my rescue as she talked about her decision to be exposed as well. She said, "My decision to expose myself to the sexism of Dr. Dre, Ice Cube, Snoop Dogg, or the Notorious B.I.G. is really my plea to my brothers to tell me who they are. I need to know why they are so angry at me. Why is disrespecting me one of the few things that make them feel like men? What's the haps, what are you going through on the daily that's got you acting so foul?"[10] Morgan points us in the direction of the question at hand: how do we embrace the contradictions implicit in male hip-hop artists' affirming women on one hand and degrading women on the other hand? How do we deal with these contradictions in an engaging and constructive manner? Morgan suggests that we look at the pain in the story that on the surface is insulting and degrading. While critiquing the culture, we need to look at the *why* question. Why does hip-hop culture perpetuate the sexist, violent, and misogynistic views of American culture? What is really going on in the hearts and minds of artists who step up to the microphone and degrade women and speak of killing one another while consuming drugs as if they were candy? Morgan goes on to say:

> As a black woman and a feminist I listen to the music with a willingness to see past the machismo in order to be clear about what I'm *really* dealing with. What I hear frightens me. On booming track after booming track, I hear brothers talking about spending each day high as hell on malt liquor and Chronic. Don't sleep. What passes for "40 and a blunt" good times in most of hip-hop is really alcoholism, substance abuse, and chemical dependency. When brothers can talk so cavalierly about killing each other

and then reveal that they have no expectation to see their twenty-first birthday, that is straight-up depression *masquerading* as machismo.[11]

Morgan is on to something here. She has given us a different set of ears to listen with. What do we really hear as the culture spews lyrics and images that are offensive to our Christian sensibilities? Do we hear the pain? Do we hear the words and condemn the artist, or do we hear an artist who is just as confused and conflicted as we are as we listen? Morgan does not excuse the culture; rather, she engages the culture. She sees something that many miss because they are so quick to judge the culture rather than learn from it. What are these artists trying to cover up? What is prompting them to do what they do and say what they say? What context are they coming from that produces lyrics that speak of attacking women and their brothers? What are the sociocontextual buttons that drive hip-hop to promote death among its members?

Morgan goes on to talk about how she used her new pair of hip-hop feminist ears to hear the Notorious B.I.G.'s first album, *Ready to Die*. This is what she says about the album that chronicles the life, times, and struggles of B.I.G. to this point:

> We boarded with the story of his birth, strategically stopped to view his dysfunctional, warring family, his first robbery, his first stint in jail, murder, drug-dealing, getting paid, partying, sexin', rappin', mayhem, and death. Biggie's player persona might have momentarily convinced the listener that he was livin' phat without a care in the world but other moments divulged his inner hell. The chorus of "Everyday Struggle": *I don't wanna live no more/Sometimes I hear death knockin' at my front door* revealed that "Big Poppa" was also plunged with guilt, regret, and depression. The album ultimately ended in his suicide.[12]

B.I.G. really is suicidal. He is sexist, and we don't want to miss or excuse his sexism, but we must not miss his brokenness. He is a man who has not learned how to love his momma or his baby's momma. He is a man who is lost and trying to find his way via an industry that capitalizes on and promotes his brokenness for profit. In the final analysis, Biggie the Playa is being played. This doesn't excuse him from his role in this melodrama, but it helps us look beyond the obvious. To quote Morgan again, "The seemingly impenetrable wall of sexism in rap music is really the complex mask African-Americans often wear both to hide and express pain. . . . Hip-hop is still one of the few forums in which young black men, even surreptitiously, are allowed to express their pain. . . . It's extremely telling that men who can only see us as 'bitches' and 'hos' refer to themselves as 'niggas.'"[13] Hip-hop wears a mask that grins and lies. It is a mask that takes us to the place where the culture says out loud what it is thinking. This shouldn't be excused, but it must be engaged. The presented problem is a window to the real problem. Something is going on, and the fan and the student of hip-hop must lean in and listen with hip-hop feminist ears that critique, correct, and get at the root of the problem. Hip-hop must be held accountable, but we have to ask for what we are holding it accountable.

Track 5: Pimps Up, Hos Down: When Hip-Hop Goes Too Far

After saying all of that and agreeing with and extending Joan Morgan's assessment, I feel there is still more to say. With the risk of being redundant, I have to invoke Michael Dyson here. As I talk about when hip-hop culture simply goes too far, let me ward off the critics of hip-hop who will underline this part of the book. Dyson says:

> Hip-hop critics make a valid point that the genre is full of problematic expressions. It reeks of materialism; it feeds on stereotypes and offensive language; it spoils with retrogressive views; it is rife with hedonism; and it surely doesn't always side with humanistic values. But the arguments of many of hip-hop's critics demand little engagement with hip-hop. Their views don't require much beyond attending to surface symptoms of a culture that offers far more depth and color when it's taken seriously and criticized thoughtfully.[14]

In agreement with Dyson, I want to suggest that when hip-hop goes too far—and it does—it still demands a thoughtful engagement. The words that create the culture and the culture itself must be taken seriously in the critique. Not only that, but the critique must also contextualize the culture. Hip-hop didn't fall from the sky, and it isn't produced in a vacuum. Critiques of hip-hop must also take into account the capitalist culture that contributes to its production. This doesn't let hip-hop culture off the hook; it simply places the critique in a broader frame.

Hip-hop wears a mask that grins and lies. It is a mask that takes us to the place where the culture says out loud what it is thinking. This shouldn't be excused, but it must be engaged.

I agree with Dyson that hip-hop has its problems. We can't skirt these problems. We must address them head-on. As much as I agree with Joan Morgan when she says that hip-hop takes us into the thoughts of young men, I can't excuse those thoughts or the images they produce. Hip-hop must be held accountable for what it contributes in the way of sexist, misogynistic, violent, abusive images and realities. Hip-hop can't get a hall pass. Hip-hop has to be brought into the classroom, studied, understood, and engaged at the deepest levels. Yes, parts of hip-hop culture reek with materialism. Other parts are indeed offensive and feed stereotypes. While confessing the bad in hip-hop, let me also say that hip-hop can't be blamed for everything. As Dyson says in reference to the Don Imus comments that caused a stir in 2007:

> It is a red herring to suggest hip-hop's undeniable virulence toward black females as a justification for the bleak antipathy toward black women that grips mainstream

American culture. White culture venomously attacked black women long before the birth of hip-hop, which helps explain Imus's beliefs. It is entirely tragic that hip-hop has done more than its share to disseminate such madness toward black females. In fact, hip-hop has made the assault on black women stylish and perhaps more acceptable by supplying linguistic updates (like the word "ho") to deeply entrenched bigotry.[15]

Yes, hip-hop has contributed to the problems of sexism, homophobia, violence, and misogyny; but hip-hop didn't invent them. In the quotation above, Dyson strikes the balance that is necessary. He doesn't withdraw or lighten his critique, but he doesn't blame hip-hop for Imus's comments. Hip-hop can't be blamed for the ills of society. If hip-hop is blamed for the ills of society, then we've given too much power to hip-hop, and that has deep sociological and theological implications. The truth of the matter is that hip-hop is a part of the larger culture, and hip-hop, like the larger popular culture, must be engaged, critiqued, and looked at objectively.

Track 6: Push It: Women in Hip-Hop

Hip-hop culture can be a catch-22 for women. I don't claim to speak for women, but I do want to try to hear their concerns when it comes to hip-hop culture. Women who are a part of hip-hop culture are in a difficult place. How can they be a part of a culture that portrays them narrowly and how do they promote and/or resist these portrayals? Patricia Hill Collins says that the "theme of the materialistic, sexualized Black woman has become an icon within hip-hop culture. The difficulty lies in telling the difference between representations of Black women who are sexually liberated and those who are sexual objects."[16] Artists like Li'l Kim are at one extreme of the continuum, and Missy Elliot is at the other. Li'l Kim flaunts her body and sexuality, and Missy Elliot almost dismisses hers. They both have been criticized, with Li'l Kim bearing the brunt of public outcry for her sexual politics. Then there was Shawnaa's song "Gettin' Some," in which she brags about a man doing to her what most men brag about women doing to them (oral sex) in their songs. Shawnaa came under attack for bragging about what men talk about all the time. How do women become a part of hip-hop culture when the rules aren't the same for them? Male artists rap about abusing and using the bodies of women for male enjoyment, and women's bodies have become icons in hip-hop culture, but women are prohibited from or critiqued for taking control of their bodies and images. As Dyson says:

> When you survey the landscape, here's what you get: the extension of crotch politics of black machismo; the subordination of female desire to male desire; the recolonizing of the black female body by the imperialistic gaze of the black male. Black men want to dominate women according to their own sexual desire. They issue sexual edicts about bodies of women who come within their circle of influence. The price of

admission in that culture is a surrender of sexual autonomy by the women in order to please the desire of men.[17]

This is the struggle women face. How do they get into the culture when men are at the door controlling who gets in and defining the terms for participation? Female artists from Remy Ma to Shawnaa to Li'l Kim to Foxy Brown have to come in via the door that is controlled by men. At the same time, the sexual politics of the larger culture have influenced hip-hop, and what we see in the larger culture we now see in hip-hop. "In other words, it ain't hip-hop that's teaching the broader culture how to dog a woman; it's the broader culture's ways and rules that are keyed in by hip-hop."[18] This doesn't excuse hip-hop, but it does help us to contextualize the widespread cultural abuse and exploitation of women and to realize that we have to address the deep, large, and pervasive roots of sexism.

When women use their bodies in the production of hip-hop culture it highlights the issue Patricia Hill Collins pointed out: are these women liberating themselves and taking control of their image and the definition of sexuality in the culture, or are they contributing to the objectification of women? This is a part of the critique we must make as we view hip-hop culture as art and cultural production. How are women being used, for what purpose, and who is in control? When I watch Eve's video "Tambourine," I am not as offended as when I watch Will.I.Am's "I Got It from My Mamma." In Eve's video, she appears to be in control of her image. She is not the backdrop for a man's exploitive purpose. The video is provocative but tasteful. In Will.I.Am's video, the woman is a tool for his male, sexist exploitation. While the song is cute, the images are troubling. As Collins says:

> Objectifying Black women's bodies turns them into canvases that can be interchanged for a variety of purposes. Historically, this objectification had a clear racial motive. In the post–civil rights era, however, this use of Black women's bodies also has a distinctive gender subtext. . . . African American men who star in music videos construct a certain version of manhood against the backdrop of objectified nameless, quasi naked Black women who populate their stage. At the same time, African American women in these same videos often objectify their own bodies in order to be accepted within this Black male-controlled universe.[19]

This universe of hip-hop, which is controlled by men, must be challenged. This debate will continue; questions about women's roles and the power of these roles in hip-hop culture have to be a part of the critique of hip-hop culture. (I extend this conversation in chap. 7.)

Track 7: Hustlin': Brothas and Sistas Caught in the Middle

In 2004 Nelly was scheduled to perform at Spelman College in an effort to raise awareness of his sister's need for a bone marrow transplant. The appearance was set, but the sisters on campus had had enough and they called Nelly on the carpet for sexist lyrics and degrading images of women in his videos. (For example, his video for "Tip Drill" shows a woman's buttocks used to swipe a credit card as if she and her body were for sale.) The show was canceled.

This is a famous story, but what are brothers and sisters to do? Do they stop listening? Do they buy a controversial artist's album and skip the "bad" songs? Do they buy edited CDs—now that the cursing is gone is the moral of the story different? When at a club, do they exit the dance floor when a particular song comes on? What about getting a revelation in the middle of the song on the dance floor? Take one of the famous club songs, "Get Low," by Lil Jon.[20] Later in my life, I started to DJ as a way of getting into and becoming hip-hop. So I found myself in my mid-thirties DJing hip-hop parties for teens and college students. As a DJ, I know that "Get Low" packs the floor. But the song is very troubling. What do I do with this? When I am in the club or at a party DJing and I drop this song, the dance floor swells. I have even caught feminists (men and women) dancing to this song. I have caught myself dancing to this song. When I want to move the crowd at a party, I know the songs that will move the crowd usually talk about body parts in a way that is troubling, but I play them. What are we to do about this?

Do we continue to endorse, listen to, and participate in a male-dominated culture? Maybe men and women need to stand up and be a vocal part of the critical engagement with hip-hop culture. I don't know the answer, but I do know that being a part of hip-hop culture demands that we ask the questions and confess these moments of confusion. I don't know if we have to stop dancing. I don't know if I will ever stop playing Lil Jon because as a DJ I am trying to get people to dance, but I am still in a quandary.

I remember one night when my wife accompanied me to a dance. She had never heard the Ying Yang Twins' song "Wait." When I dropped that song, she looked at me like I was crazy. She demanded that I turn it off. When I looked out at the dance floor, I saw all the college students repeating the words and doing their thing. At the end of the night, my wife and I talked about it. I defended the creativity of the whisper they used, which was new back then, and she critiqued the vulgarity of the song. I agreed with everything she said, but I still said, "It is a good song!" I was talking about the artistic expression and what made the song good art. She was talking about the vulgar words and images the song put forth. We both were right, and we continue to hold these two views in conflict.

We are caught in the middle looking both ways. We look at the good, the bad, and the vulgar. To engage hip-hop, we have to look at all sides and from all perspectives. We need to conduct an intelligent, well-informed critique. The critique is warranted, but even the bad may contain a story that we need to hear. In the end, we have to listen to, watch, and learn from the culture. This starts with intense lyrical analysis.

At times, I have been listening to songs, bouncing my head, when all of a sudden I ask myself what I am saying. This revelation or moment of shock comes when a song gets stuck in my head and I find myself repeating the lyrics under my breath. This often happens when the song is out of context, meaning I am not at a club or DJing a party. I'm riding in my car or listening in my office. When I have this type of experience, I go directly to the lyrics to try to figure out what the song is about. What is the story that got me to this chorus? Step one is being conscious of what we are listening to. Then we can't be afraid to be in the middle and appear conflicted. This is who we are as we listen to and to some extent become hip-hop. We have to take time to be reflective.

This morning I got up and put on Jay Z's classic *Reasonable Doubt*. This album was recorded in 1997, but it is still as fresh as ever. I am still listening to hip-hop. As I write, I am bouncing my head up and down, caught in a moment of joy. As Jay Z says, you got to respect the hustle. I respect the hustle of hip-hop culture. Hip-hop is ours, and we are hip-hop. Let's ride together and keep the conversation going between the tracks. Ride with me because my Bose system is rockin'. I want some more!

Getting in Touch with Hip-Hop

Albums

Brown Sugar, music from the motion picture soundtrack. MCA, 2002.
Common. *Be*. GOOD/Geffen, 2005.
————. *Finding Forever*. GOOD/Geffen, 2007.
————. *One Day It'll All Make Sense*. Relativity, 1997.
Mos Def. *Black on Both Sides*. Rawkus, 1999.
Notorious B.I.G, The. *Ready to Die*. Bad Boy, 1994.

Books

Kool Moe Dee. *There's a God on the Mic: The True 50 Greatest MCs*. New York: Thunder's Mouth Press, 2003.
Morgan, Joan. *When Chickenheads Come Home to Roost: My Life as a Hip-Hop Feminist*. New York: Simon & Schuster, 1999.

Films

The Art of 16 Bars. Directed by Peter Spirer. QD3 Entertainment, 2005.
Brown Sugar. Directed by Rick Famuyiwa. Fox Searchlight, 2002.

5

"slippin' and slidin' i'm about to give up"

The Theological Truth in the Story

Who Listens to DMX?

Nastasia Watkins came into our lives on April 10, 1986; she was our firstborn child. My wife, Vanessa, and I knew from the start that she would have something to say; she came out of her mother's womb talkin' noise. As she grew, we learned from this beautiful child who would become fully hip-hop. As her teenage years approached, we braced ourselves, and the bracing was warranted. In 1998, when DMX came out with his first full-length album, *It's Dark and Hell Is Hot*, Nastasia used her allowance to buy it. She blasted it from her room—mind you, the unedited version. Here I was, the professor and minister, saying, "Could you please close your door or at least turn it down." Instead of acquiescing to my request, she said, "Daddy, you really ought to listen to DMX; he tells the truth." "He tells the truth" is what she said. What caught me was her conviction about DMX and her embrace of what she saw as authenticity and truth in his music. I took her advice, and we listened together. Nastasia and I would eventually conduct workshops around DMX in the local church. What Nastasia heard in the story as told by DMX is what draws people to him and artists like him. They see an authenticity, a realness, a story that doesn't shy away from the contradictions and complexities of life.

After I finished a Bible study series on DMX in the fall of 2008, I was sitting down with the leaders of the young adult ministry at dinner. Terrell said, "Doc, you ended the DMX series too soon. He spoke to me like no one else. You can feel him when he raps. He is so honest. You can almost see him going through his life struggles as he prays and raps. I got so much from X." Here I was in the local church almost ten years after my daughter confronted me with DMX, and I was hearing the same thing. What is it about DMX that speaks so loud to so many? What is the truth that comes out of the mouth of DMX? Is God speaking through DMX? Is this the weeping prophet?

The word of the LORD came to me, saying,

"Before I formed you in the womb I knew you,
before you were born I set you apart;
I appointed you as a prophet to the nations."

"Alas, Sovereign LORD," I said, "I do not know how to speak; I am too young."

But the LORD said to me, "Do not say, 'I am too young.' You must go to everyone I send you to and say whatever I command you. Do not be afraid of them, for I am with you and will rescue you," declares the LORD.

Then the LORD reached out his hand and touched my mouth and said to me, "Now, I have put my words in your mouth. See, today I appoint you over nations and kingdoms to uproot and tear down, to destroy and overthrow, to build and to plant." (Jer. 1:4–10)

What if God is using DMX as his weeping prophet? What if God is calling DMX to uproot and tear down, to destroy and overthrow, to build and to plant? The thing that hit me about Nastasia's comments in 1998 and Terrell's comments in 2007 is that I hear the same thing about DMX all the time: he speaks truth. For me truth is no light concept. When I hear the truth as spoken word, my mind goes to that famous prayer in John 17:

My prayer is not that you take them out of the world but that you protect them from the evil one. They are not of the world, even as I am not of it. Sanctify them by the truth; your word is truth. As you sent me into the world, I have sent them into the world. For them I sanctify myself, that they too may be truly sanctified. (vv. 15–19)

A couple things in this passage resonate with what I hear when I talk with fans of DMX. The first thing Jesus prayed was that his people not come out of the world but that the Father might protect them from the evil one in the world. The issue of protection from evil is central in the words of DMX. Second, Jesus says that somehow the word as spoken by God through him—and I would add, others—is truth and that this truth sanctifies because words that are given by God are words of truth. This is connected with that famous passage in John 8:32: "Then you will know the truth, and the truth will set you free." In this passage, Jesus claims that if you hold to his teaching or his word, which is truth, you are·

his disciples, and this truth has a way of freeing you. If God is speaking through DMX and DMX is speaking truth, then what Nastasia, Terrell, and countless others get from DMX is truth that sets them free.

DMX: the weeping prophet, telling stories that make us shout

Track 1: Can the Words of DMX Be a Type of Sacred Text or Word That Sets People Free?

We have to start with this question: what is scripture? Wilfred Cantwell Smith says, "No text is a scripture in itself and as such. People—a given community— make a text into scripture, or keep it scripture: by treating it in a certain way. I suggest: *scripture is a human activity*."[1] In the community of those who listen to DMX, the question is, if DMX's words are seen as truth, are they elevated to the status of a type of scripture? We don't have sufficient space in this book to report the findings to such a question, but it is still a concept we have to wrestle with. How are the words of DMX elevated to a type of sacred text or sacred truthful word by those who listen and by the claims of DMX as he asserts that God speaks through him?

William Graham says, "A text becomes 'scripture' in active, subjective relationship to persons, and as part of a cumulative communal tradition. No text, written or oral or both, is sacred or authoritative in isolation from a community."[2] Therefore, it is in the context of a community that a text becomes sacred. In this context, we could also say that a word that is elevated to a type of sacred text is spoken before it is written. As Graham says:

The generative power of the spoken word is apparently one of the most basic and widespread of religious themes. . . . Speech always precedes writing, cosmically and anthropologically as well as historically. If there is anything that can be called protoscripture, it is surely the utterances of ecstatics, prophets, and seers, in which it is commonly held to be not they but the divinity who speaks through them as their chosen mouthpieces.[3]

DMX claims that he is being used by God. DMX becomes one of God's seers who speaks on behalf of God to God's children. In his rap and prayers, which we will analyze later in this chapter, DMX makes the explicit claim that he is a mouthpiece for God, that he does what he does for God. In hip-hop culture, as in other societies, truth is bound up in the spoken word. "In virtually every society, truth is bound up in significant ways with the spoken word, whether the word is that of a divinity or that of a human sage or teacher. . . . Here also, one still has to learn from others, and not insignificantly through oral means."[4] In hip-hop culture, the words of the emcee, as he or she becomes seer, prophet, and teacher, are of central importance. The emcee's role morphs from artist into one assigned by the divine. The emcee becomes a teacher sent by God.

The role of emcee as revealer of truth is inexplicably tied to the authenticity of the teacher, which is linked to his or her story. In the case of DMX, his story of struggle and hard times—which is a very public story—gives him credibility in hip-hop culture. DMX's story isn't a made-up studio story, and DMX credits God for bringing him through his hard times for the purpose of saving others by telling the truth. Graham says, "Knowledge or truth, especially salvific knowledge or truth, is tied to the living words of authentic persons, not authentic documents. Further, these living words can be valid only on the lips of one who has been given authority from a valid teacher to use them."[5] The valid authority in the case of DMX is God. It is also the community who has affirmed and celebrated the truth in his story by embracing his message as a communal message of salvation. Those who embrace DMX's story as truth are set free by the story they listen to, internalize, and feel as they recite, memorize, and own the words of DMX as their words.

Central to hip-hop culture is an embrace of hip-hop lyrics. Members of the hip-hop nation know the words to the raps. They recite them at concerts and on buses, earbuds firmly placed in their ears. The eardrum is linked to the heartbeat that moves the spirit of the hip-hop devotee. The words, as they are repeated over and over again, take on a meaning internalized by the hip-hop devotee. "Meaning is carried by the recitation over and above the particular meaning of the literal passage recited, however deeply felt and understood that meaning may be on an intellectual plane. How to get at that meaning," says Graham, which also applies here, "is a detailed project for another place,"[6] but we must recognize that there is something going on as one recites raps over and over to the point of memory and these raps become embodied in the listener. As Graham goes on to say, "Memorization is a particularly intimate appropriation of a text, and the capacity to quote or recite a text from memory is a spiritual resource that is tapped automatically in every act of reflection, worship, prayer, or moral deliberation, as well as in times of personal and communal decision or crisis."[7] The listener becomes a part of what is said by the teacher, sent by God, in the form of an emcee. The listener comes to own the lyrics as much as they were first owned by the emcee. When listeners memorize a rap and repeat it over and over again, it is essentially *in* them. The word becomes flesh as it dwells in them. It becomes a holy word as it holds them, sustains them, and lives in their whole being.

To claim the centrality of the spoken word as a sacred word isn't new. What the emcee is doing in hip-hop culture is an old standard in the religious culture. "The spoken word of scripture has been overwhelmingly the most important medium through which religious persons and groups throughout history have known and interacted with sacred texts. Most of those myriad persons who have claimed a sacred text all have received, known, and transmitted its message orally, not in writing."[8] In the context of hip-hop culture, the emcee claims a status of being sent by God that is affirmed by the community, and his or her words take on an elevated, sacred status. As those in the hip-hop community search for authenticity and truth, they do not center this discussion on the Bible. In essence, "the Bible has lost much of its earlier widely recognized stature as the only textual authority transcending national boundaries, sectarian divisions, ethnic or cultural diversities, and differences of socio-economic or intellectual class. . . . Once a generally recognized locus of contact with things transcendent, the Bible has undergone a 'leveling.'"[9] This leveling of the Bible as the only sacred text has been balanced by the sacred words of emcees who speak truth out of a story that is true. These truths, as words from God to set God's people free, serve to liberate those who hear them. The truth is in the story as told by the emcee as he or she is used by God.

In the context of hip-hop culture, the emcee claims a status of being sent by God that is affirmed by the community, and his or her words take on an elevated, sacred status.

Track 2: *It's Dark and Hell Is Hot*: Truth in the Struggle of the Story

DMX burst on to the national hip-hop scene with his guest appearance on Mase's album *Harlem World* in 1997. The voice of DMX rang out on the song "24 Hours to Live" as a dog barking in the night. The voice was gruff, with the power of Tupac and the clarity of the Notorious B.I.G. While the rap world was grieving the deaths of Tupac Shakur (1971–96) and the Notorious B.I.G. (1972–97), DMX appeared as heir apparent. DMX followed his guest appearance on Mase's album with the release of his single "Get at Me Dog" in early 1998. Riding the success of the smash single, DMX debuted at number one on the pop charts with his album *It's Dark and Hell Is Hot* in late 1998. In his first full-length album, DMX captured the beauty and pain of inner-city life. His tragic life story served as the text for the exegesis of struggle, pain, and liberation. He followed his debut with three successful albums. In the corpus of his work, we see a socio-rap-theologian asking and answering religious questions. Many fans referred to DMX as "the Preacher." On each album, he openly prayed, blurring the lines between sacred and secular. When we listen to DMX and reflect on the images he gave us through his videos and movies, we are able to gain a deeper insight into our understanding of the Bible. For example, as I will show, DMX can help us gain a deeper understanding of the Joseph story.

DMX's life is one of suffering, pain, and liberation. He spent most of his childhood in and out of group homes and juvenile institutions. As a young adult, he did several stints in prison while trying to find his way. A petty thief who was abused by his mother and left by his father, he raised himself in Yonkers, New York, and he discovered early on that his pain was his gift. The gift was the story his life had given him, and he would go on to use that story to inform his own brand of socio-rap-theology. He would come to understand that his story was not simply one of personal testimony but also one to which inner-city African Americans could testify. The witness of DMX rang true, for it was a truth that came out of struggle. DMX's story also captivated those who did not live his life story but listened in as voyeurs. The gift of his story and his ability to retell it in the form of rap became his means of public catharsis. His pain became the road map for his future as well as a balm for those who heard his story and could relate to it.

The rap music of DMX is spiritual, cathartic, redemptive, and religious. His gruff and gritty style reflects the harshness of inner-city life for working-class, urban Americans. The stories he weaves over the hard beats enable the listeners to feel his story. When his work is translated to video, the circle is complete. You can feel, hear, see, and enter his world while empathizing with so many who have shared similar struggles. The claim James Cone made for the blues we now make for the music of DMX: "The blues are secular spirituals. They are *secular* in the sense that they confine their attention solely to the immediate and affirm the bodily expression of black soul, including its sexual manifestations. They are *spirituals* because they are impelled by the same search for the truth of the black experience."[10] DMX deals with the immediate struggle of what it means to be young, African American, male, and working-poor in America in the late-twentieth century—and now in the early twenty-first century. DMX also seeks to unearth the truth of his experience and the experiences of those like him who are seeking answers in the spiritual dimension of their lives. Therefore, like the blues, the rap of DMX

can be seen as secular spirituals dealing with the immediate while simultaneously searching for spiritual truths.

To fully understand and appreciate the work of DMX, it is important to think
about music in the context of theomusicology. Jon Michael Spencer defines
theomusicology:

> Unlike ethnomusicology, whose practitioners view religion as a compartmentalized
> part of culture, theomusicologists view religion as all-pervasive in culture. We view
> religion as all-pervasive insofar as culture is created by human beings whom we
> understand to be inescapably religious. In this regard, religious human beings are
> those who naturally ask and ponder myriad vital questions that arise out of our sense
> of finiteness. These are questions that ultimately can never be answered by us except
> provisionally, given that we are not omniscient like God. What we tend not to realize,
> however, is that the vital questions that comprise a part of the discourse of secular
> popular music are the same for which institutionalized religious places provide canon-
> ized answers—the church, temple, synagogue, and mosque.[11]

DMX's brand of hip-hop raises religious questions in the context of his lived
experience while appealing to God for answers. His work is clearly a reflection of
what Spencer calls religious in that he is asking the big questions and providing
honest answers while simultaneously recognizing his finiteness. He struggles
with life more honestly than established religious traditions because he is not
bound by the dogma or doctrines of any tradition. He is free to explore and
reflect without the limitations of a denomination. Theological reflection in this
type of music is more authentic than what we find in music we categorize as
religious. Spencer puts it this way:

> In fact there seems to be something inauthentic about church music in general: it is
> perhaps doctrinally "correct" but not actually reflective of people's beliefs and behav-
> iors in the real world. In other words, if we really want to know what the masses are
> thinking religiously—the Christian slaveholder or the skinhead rock and roller—we
> cannot turn to church music, where provisional answers to the vital questions are
> already narrowly predetermined. We must turn to the secular sphere outside the
> institutional sacred gathering places, where a more honest religious discourse—no
> matter how "profane" it may be—is occurring.[12]

To truly know what the masses are thinking religiously, we turn to hip-hop
music and artists like DMX, a socio-rap-theologian honestly raising rich theological questions and then providing provisional answers as he continues his
quest with his listeners for answers.

Track 3: Looking Back at the Word through the Word

DMX's story is the cultural expression we use to reverse the hermeneutic. The
model of Larry Kreitzer is used here for what he has called "reversing the her-

meneutical flow." Kreitzer contends that we learn more about the biblical text as we use "enduring expressions of our own culture" to reexamine or exegete the biblical text.[13] This is a process of reading back to the text as we interpret the text from our present context and ask what it has to say today or what is missing in the text. As we reverse the hermeneutical flow, we start with the present cultural expression and read the text looking for meaning, application, connection, and exegetical relationship to the present. Other forms of biblical criticism are not dismissed in this process but rather extended. In this case, DMX adds to the interpretive theological lens as we use his socio-theological lens to reclaim the Joseph story for working-class, inner-city African Americans. We can use the cultural production of DMX from 1998 to 2001 along with his autobiography (published in 2003) and interviews published in popular magazines as vehicles by which to read the text.

The Joseph story is one of alienation and pain. Joseph has to learn how to live in a desperate situation while holding on to his dreams. When Joseph shares his dreams with his brothers, he is rejected and sold into slavery. He eventually finds himself in prison. For DMX, the parallels of dreaming, being ostracized, and then finding himself in prison are amazingly similar to the story of Joseph. When you take the stories of DMX, of working-class, inner-city African Americans, and of Joseph and put them in dialogue, the rich contours of similarity weave together into a tapestry of struggle. If modern-day socio-theologians want to better understand the Joseph story, they should read the Joseph story through the eyes of DMX and the millions of working poor in America who live in a country that offers a dream that seems inaccessible to them. This is DMX's story—one in which he fights to achieve a dream while his brothers in the 'hood are hatin' on him. DMX tries to believe in himself, his dreams, and his gifts, while his mother, like Joseph's father, doesn't know what to do with a child who dares to dream of greatness. DMX dreams and pursues his dreams amid difficult circumstances, and he faces each obstacle with both doubt and courage. This is the insight DMX gives us that is missing from the biblical text of the Joseph story. The doubt of Joseph isn't revealed in the biblical text. Joseph is painted as a young man who moves on and moves up with no doubt or struggle, but we know better. DMX reveals his struggles; he reveals his doubts; he reveals his issues with God, his insecurities, and his pain. When we read the biblical text in light of DMX's lyrics and life story, not only do we see things we wouldn't see, but the story actually comes to life.

What DMX is doing in his work is engaging in what Anthony Pinn has labeled nitty-gritty hermeneutics. According to Pinn, "Nitty-gritty hermeneutics is an exercise which, through additional discourse and exploration, promises a deeper understanding of Black religious thought and its various responses to suffering—the problem of evil. Nitty-gritty hermeneutics and its interpretative roughness free inquiry from the restrictions posed by 'theodicy.'"[14] Pinn goes on to say that "nitty-gritty hermeneutics surfacing in the blues interprets religion, based upon complex Black life, as a tool by which humans are encouraged to remove psychologically comforting theological crutches and develop themselves as liberators."[15]

DMX's music embodies the principles of nitty-gritty hermeneutics. Even though he appeals to African American religious ethics and references Christianity as an influence in his theology, he is free from the constraints of any religious system. As Pinn puts it, for "rap artists and their predecessors—the blues singers—songs are not couched in psychologically comforting language. Rather, their interpretation or perceptions are raw and unpolished. In this way, they illustrate the intent, function, and operation of nitty-gritty hermeneutics."[16] The rawness, realness, and honesty of DMX as he tells his story while raising theological questions are at the heart of this discussion.

Track 4: A Man Who Never Was a Boy

It's Dark and Hell Is Hot is the title of DMX's first full-length album. On the track "Look thru My Eyes," he says, "I bare my soul," and this he does. In the chorus of the song, DMX invites listeners to look through his eyes and see what he sees; in essence, listeners are invited to participate in his world, to live in his world through his music and videos. We are in his world seeing the struggles, pains, and joys of DMX. He cries to the listening participants to feel his pain as he shouts that he was a man who never really had a childhood.

The boy DMX (Earl Simmons) was misunderstood because of his complex life circumstances and brilliance. At age ten, he began his long relationship with penal institutions. The boy was ten years old and a student at School 18 when he had to become a man. He was told he couldn't return to his school the next year. He was sent before a judge. "The judge told my mother that since she was incapable of keeping me out of trouble, the courts had to intervene and so I was sent to Julia Dyckman Andrus Children's Home, a school/dormitory facility about twenty minutes away from our house. The term was eighteen months."[17] This was the first officially recorded rejection and incarceration of DMX. His mother couldn't take care of him. His father wasn't in the home. DMX felt isolated. The judge sent him to a home that never became a home. The plight of being isolated, rejected, and sent to the next penal institution became a way of life for DMX.

DMX's experience at Andrus had a tragic end that was reminiscent of what happened at School 18. He and his roommate started a fire. DMX was held accountable for the fire and after getting in a fight with his roommate was banished to solitary confinement and eventually put out of Andrus. When you read DMX's account of his first stint in incarceration, which led to deeper hurt and pain, you grasp the call he issues in "Look thru My Eyes." You see a child who is looking for love and affirmation from an absent father and a mother who isn't prepared to give him the love he needs and wants. He is left alone, put out of his house, and as a result he acts out. His anger, pain, and hurt turn in on him. The violent outbursts and socially unacceptable behavior come as a result of his own pain. All the while the boy who is being locked up is trying to hold on to the dream, to fulfill what he understands as his destiny: to be a great artist one day.

Prison—being sold or taken away from your family—isn't a vacation. The Bible story of Joseph fails to show the reader the emotions and feelings of Joseph. In Genesis 37:1–11, the Bible provides a picture of a young man who shares his dream of greatness with his family and is scolded for his dream, not celebrated. In Genesis 37:12–36, Joseph is sold into slavery by his brothers. What was Joseph feeling? Was he hurt? Did he feel rejected? How did he process the pain of not only being rejected and misunderstood by his family but also being sold by them? The Bible fails to answer these questions, but it stands to reason that Joseph felt pain. DMX helps us answer some of these questions. He implies in the song "Look thru My Eyes" that if we had to walk in his shoes we would feel his pain. We would see what he sees, feel what he feels, and this would give us the ability to sympathize with him if not empathize with him.

Chapter 9 of DMX's autobiography tells one of the stories that was fuel for what we hear in "Look thru My Eyes." DMX tells how his mother took him to the Children's Village School for Boys under the pretense that they were only going for a visit. As the visit progressed, DMX began to feel it wasn't simply a visit. After his mother spent an hour talking with the headmaster, she emerged to tell him that he was going to stay at the home. He was in shock! His mother gave him the news she was leaving him in front of a group of children who looked on at this painful moment. DMX goes on to share how he acted out and how painful this was. When you read this story in light of "Look thru My Eyes" and then reflect on the Joseph story, can you sense how Joseph must have felt? Joseph had to be angry; he had to feel pain. DMX said, "I was in shock. I knew we were coming to a group home but I never thought my mother would drop me off at one with no warning!" "You're really going to enjoy yourself here, Earl," Mr. White said. "I could have killed that mother—— for saying that bull——, but within the hour, my mother was gone."[18] DMX was outraged. He couldn't believe his mother, someone he thought would love and protect him, would just leave him.

Joseph is sent by his father to see how his brothers are doing as they are grazing the flock. He doesn't find them in the place they are supposed to be, so he goes to Dothan, where he is told they are. He goes searching for them never thinking they will hurt him, try to kill him, or sell him into slavery. Joseph can't hear them as they make their plot, but the text tells this part of the story. If it wasn't for Reuben and Judah, who stepped in and pleaded with the other brothers not to kill Joseph, he may have wound up dead at the hands of his brothers.

DMX deals with brothers hating brothers in "Look thru My Eyes" when he says, "Burnin' in hell, but don't deserve to be, got niggas I don't even know wanna murder me, just because they heard of me." DMX is dealing with brothers who hate him and want to kill him because of his reputation. They can't accept him and his dream of being a great rapper. DMX was a dreamer like Joseph. Joseph's brothers said, "Here comes that dreamer! . . . Come now, let's kill him and throw him into one of these cisterns and say that a ferocious animal devoured him" (Gen. 37:19–20). Joseph had to be hurt when he walked into the company of his brothers and got wind of the plot. The words DMX spoke at the Children's Village School for Boys give us insight into what this feels like. I am sure Joseph would have said in unison with DMX, "I was in shock." It is painful when family leaves you. It hurts when your brothers hate you for dreaming. It hurts when those you think should love and support you turn on you. As DMX sings his songs and tells his story, he is honest about his pain. When DMX is put in dialogue with Joseph, we can begin to imagine how Joseph must have felt.

Joseph and DMX could have a conversation about what it feels like to be left by your family. Joseph walks up to his brothers and within a matter of an hour, just like DMX at the Children's Village School for Boys, is given to another family. After Joseph's brothers throw him in a cistern, they sit down to have lunch. As they are eating, they casually decide they could profit from selling their brother instead of letting him die. Ironically enough, DMX remembers that when he was taken to the Children's Village School for Boys, the boys were having lunch. It was over a meal that he was left and over a meal that Joseph was sold. The sacred time of breaking bread is blasphemed as two lives are left wanting as their loved ones abandon them. Did Joseph say, like DMX, "I was in shock"? Shock probably isn't strong enough, but when we hear Joseph through the words of DMX, we can begin to feel what he felt. Maybe DMX's songs and prayers speak where the Bible is silent.

Talking about the title of his first album, DMX says:

> I decided to call my album *It's Dark and Hell Is Hot*. It was the perfect title. The darkness described my biggest challenges; hell described the reality of the world I was living in. After all these years, was the world finally ready to hear what I was trying to say? I was starting to see some signs, but I really didn't know yet. I just knew that I was trying my best to pour twenty-seven years of my life into the world of sixteen songs and a prayer.[19]

DMX tries to tell the entire story. He isn't bound by doctrinal constraints. He is engaging in nitty-gritty hermeneutics as he tells about his struggles. He confesses the challenges he went through and the hell he dealt with. We don't hear this from Joseph. The biblical text seems to gloss over Joseph's dark and hellish moments, but as Tony Pinn has argued, hip-hop embraces the tension of struggle without restrictions. Even though DMX becomes a rap superstar, he confesses the pain of getting to the top and the pain when he arrives at the top.

Track 5: The Nightmare of the Dream

The struggle of getting to the top, and after getting there finding it a place that is dark and hellish, is worth exploring as we look at the DMX and Joseph stories. As they strive to live their dreams, the process becomes a nightmare. The achievement of their dreams means not only being left by their families but also serving time in prison. Joseph goes from being a model slave to a prisoner after being falsely accused. According to the biblical story, he doesn't say a word. The biblical story presents Joseph as accepting his unjust imprisonment as if it were just. According to Genesis 39:6–20, Joseph is falsely accused by Potiphar's wife. She tells Potiphar the lie that Joseph attacked her in an attempt to rape her. Potiphar burns with anger, and without trial or jury Joseph is thrown into prison.

DMX tries to tell the entire story. He isn't bound by doctrinal constraints. He is engaging in nitty-gritty hermeneutics as he tells about his struggles.

So much is left out of the story. In a matter of fourteen verses, Joseph moves from model slave to prisoner. What is really going on with Joseph? These moves in Joseph's life can't be as smooth as they are presented in Scripture. From verse 17 on his life is dark as hell. Being sold into slavery and then being a model slave only to be put in prison as a result of unjust circumstances had to leave questions in the mind of Joseph.

I can hear DMX saying to Joseph, "When you live you suffer, but the key is to find the meaning through the suffering." As DMX says, "I think the chosen ones are the ones that struggle more. The Lord's children always start from the dirt up. If you only start from halfway up, then you're going to know less and you're going to be worth less to Him, but there was something I had to see, that He wanted me to see, so I could be what He wanted me to be."[20] DMX sees suffering as redemptive in that the chosen ones are formed while learning and growing in the midst of the suffering. Maybe the silence of the biblical text is pointing to what Joseph learned through his suffering. The silence invites the reader to imagine what is was like for Joseph. The text doesn't force an image on the reader. Maybe there is a parallel between how Joseph and DMX understand the meaning of their suffering. The story of Joseph is one that those who are going through hard times can relate to. Maybe they can see the story as one that empowers fellow travelers to see their hard times as redemptive or as a sign of their being chosen.

DMX understands his call by God to tell this story and help people make divine sense of their suffering. DMX sees his role as an evangelist in calling people to a point of being made whole as their stories are put in dialogue. DMX says:

> The greatest gift the Lord has given me is the gift of the word, the ability to commu-
> nicate with, and I know now that I'm here to share everything I have learned. That's

why I've always said I don't want sales, I want souls. F— a sale, a sale is eleven dollars, thirteen dollars. But if you give me a soul, I've got that for life and I'm going to try my best to bring it to the right place.[21]

DMX sees his calling as a hip-hop evangelist. His suffering empowers him to relate. DMX has learned how to find meaning in his suffering. He doesn't think he would be the rapper he is if he hadn't gone through what he went through. For DMX, somehow the tragedy of his suffering leads to a place of meaning and wholeness as his story is put in dialogue with Joseph's story and the stories of others who relate to his divinely inspired words. As DMX says, the greatest gift God gave him was words, and these words become a truth that helps fellow sufferers find meaning.

Track 6: This Is for My Dogs: A Closing Prayer

"My niggaz this is for my dogs, this is for my dogs." On track fifteen of the album, DMX is clear. This work is for his dogs, those who can feel him and walk with him. This is for his boys and girls who have been hurt, who have been left by their families, who have been misunderstood because they had a dream, who have been judged because they are different. As DMX ends *It's Dark and Hell Is Hot*, he calls his dogs, or his congregation, together. In his closing prayer on this album, DMX claims that God gave him this limelight to tell the story of those in the 'hood who have struggled just like he has. He is using his gifts and fame to tell their story, bring some healing, and make a difference.[22]

The story DMX is telling is not just for his own personal catharsis. DMX says it is for his brothers and sisters in the 'hood. The story is being told to do them some good.

If there is any question where DMX gets his words from and why he is telling his story, he sums it up in his closing prayer. DMX claims that God called him and empowered him to tell this story. The story DMX is telling is not just for his own personal catharsis. DMX says it is for his brothers and sisters in the 'hood. The story is being told to do them some good. DMX doesn't vacillate concerning his claim that his words come from God and that in his story is redemption.

DMX goes on in his prayer to let us in on what he found throughout his struggle. He found the love of God, for God was with him in all he went through.[23] DMX is saying that he beat down the door to heaven in prayer. He found the love of God through prayer, and this unconditional love got him through. He never felt love like this, for his life was absent of a healthy love. His mother rejected him, his father left him, and his brothers in the 'hood wanted to kill him. He was searching for love and acceptance all his life. In this prayer, DMX says he found this love.

DMX's claim that the love of God surrounded him and protected him sheds light on the biblical concept in the Joseph story that "God was with Joseph." At every turn in Joseph's story, the biblical text emphatically declares that God was with Joseph, and the evidence was the fact that Joseph prospered in every context. Putting DMX and Joseph in dialogue sheds light on the Joseph story in that as much as Joseph saw measures of what would be considered career success, there is the implication that while others didn't show Joseph love, God loved Joseph. Joseph, like DMX, made it through the hard times by recognizing the presence and love of God. They recognized that in all their struggles God had not abandoned them. God was with Joseph, and God was with DMX.

What If God Is Using DMX and Hip-Hop?

Is God with DMX? Does God love DMX and his dogs? Is God using DMX and the words of rap as a type of sacred text, lament, or divinely inspired oral word? DMX is clear that God is using him. When DMX's words are put in dialogue with what has been accepted in the Christian tradition as the sacred text, we learn more about the text. Do the words of DMX illuminate the Bible, or are DMX's words another type of Bible? To DMX and many of his dogs, his words are from God. Words that are from God or inspired by God are in another context: they are sacred. When a pastor in the African American Christian tradition stands up in the pulpit on Sunday morning and prays, he or she claims to have a word from the Lord. Does DMX have a word from the Lord? If a sacred text begins with divinely inspired words, and if DMX's words are inspired by God, do they become a sacred text when written in the form of rap?

What do you hear when you listen to DMX? Who has the authority to decide if DMX's words are sacred or not? As I've mentioned before, if the tradition that Wilfred Cantwell Smith and others talk about is accurate, then the final word will come from the community of believers. Smith says, "No text is a scripture in itself and as such. People—a given community—make a text into scripture, or keep it scripture: by treating it in a certain way. I suggest: *scripture is a human activity*."[24] Maybe the hip-hop nation will call a council and decide on their sacred books. Maybe they already have and the council was a concert.

Getting in Touch with Hip-Hop

DMX. *Flesh of My Flesh, Blood of My Blood.* Def Jam, 1998.
———. *It's Dark and Hell Is Hot.* Def Jam, 1998.

6

god skipped past the church

A Hip-Hop Theology and a Hip-Hop Theologian

Intro: What Did God Say?

I am often challenged by my audiences when they ask, "How do you know it is God saying anything in or through hip-hop? It is an insult to God and the church that you would even propose such an idea." My response is typically, "How do you know God isn't saying anything through hip-hop?" God has a tradition of using the voices from the margins. I am reminded of the woman at the well (John 4:1–30, 39–42). Those of her day thought there was no way she would have a word from God, but she did.

Identifying a theologian in hip-hop is the next logical step in the process. Students and those who engage me as I speak about hip-hop ask, "So what does theology look like in hip-hop?" This chapter will attempt to answer that question. Theology in hip-hop is systematic in its own way: its theological system revolves around a remix. Its theological reflection, rather than falling into a neat category such as pneumatology, Christology, soteriology, ecclesiology, and so on, is more akin to what we see in black theology or what I call Africana theology. It is a theology of liberation that asks, where is God in the liberating process as those who live in the 'hood are catching hell? It is a theology that lives in real time in the real world, confronting real problems of oppression while looking back at how God has revealed himself throughout time as an agent of liberation. Hip-hop theology pushes back against institutionalized religion and its theological construction and asks how it is a part of the liberating process. When you listen to theological reflection in hip-hop, you hear the liberating voice of God as artists ask hard questions and live with tentative answers.

A systematic theology in hip-hop is a theological reflection that is orderly and theologically rational to those in the believing community. Theology in this context is defined as thought and conversation that reflect on the divine nature and acts of God in the context of the hip-hop culture. Gordon Lynch talks about theology in the context of popular culture:

> It is concerned with questions about the nature of truth, what constitutes a meaningful view of life, what it means to live good and fulfilling lives and to build just and peaceable communities. . . . Theology involves exploring these questions in relation to the possibility of an absolute reference point to life which might inform how we think about truth, meaning, goodness, and justice.[1]

On Talib Kweli's album *Eardrum*, we hear theological reflection as Kweli raises questions about the nature of truth and what it means to have a good life.[2] Theology in the hip-hop community becomes systematic as it deals with these big questions as identified by Lynch and answered by Kweli.

A systematic theology in hip-hop is a theological reflection that is orderly and theologically rational to those in the believing community. Theology in this context is defined as thought and conversation that reflect on the divine nature and acts of God in the context of the hip-hop culture.

In the seventeen tracks on *Eardrum*, along with the three bonus tracks, we hear a contextualized hip-hop theology. While all the tracks will not be sampled here, you should listen to the entire album to get a full hearing of Kweli's worldview. Kweli wrote in the liner notes, "I speak of God often in my music, because we all try to achieve a greater understanding." Kweli goes on to say, "Of course, first and foremost, all praises and accolades are forwarded to the Most High, our creator, the spirit that connects us." Kweli's talking about God in his music isn't a coincidence or an afterthought. He sees God as the one who inspires him and is the creative force behind his work and theological reflection. It is God who gives Kweli, his listeners, and his followers an understanding of what is going on around them. God speaks to them along their journey. As Kweli writes, raps, and reflects theologically, he engages in what Will Coleman calls "tribal talk." According to Coleman, tribal talk "is committed to the future. It is a way of doing theology within a post-Christian, pluralistic, and post-modern reality. . . . It realizes that African

American spirituality, both non-Christian and Christian, is that which sustains all generations via God's life-giving spirit."[3] Kweli appeals to God's life-giving spirit as he models for us the way in which hip-hop does theology—a theology that is life-giving and sustains its listeners.

Kweli serves as a hip-hop theologian in that he is intentional about developing his theology. He says that he and his followers are seeking understanding. When I was a student in seminary back in the 1980s, we referred to theological reflection with the phrase from Augustine: "faith seeking understanding." Is Kweli leading a theological conversation in his work as his faith seeks understanding? If he is leading a theological conversation, can he be classified as a theologian? After all, who anoints theologians? Is it God, or is it the academy, or is it the institutional church? One of my early fights in the academy was my insistence on calling the people I bumped into on the streets theologians. I called my grandmamma and my granddaddy theologians. I called my pastor, who served us at St. Lawrence African Methodist Episcopal Church in Eatonville, Florida, a theologian. So today we can say that Talib Kweli is a theologian.

Focus Features/Photofest

Talib Kweli: the hip-hop theologian

As a socio-theologian, I argue that theology is divinely inspired reflection that happens in the real world by real people on the ground in community. The Holy Spirit inspires reflection as we ask God-questions in the context of our lived reality. It is through this dialogue between God's Spirit and our reality that we arrive at tentative theological conclusions. On the album *Eardrum*, Kweli proposes tentative answers that he claims to have heard from God in the context of the hip-hop community. You hear him asking God-questions—big questions that are directed at God, for only God can answer them. In chapter 5, we looked at how hip-hop has inspired its own type of sacred text in a world in which the word becomes flesh. In this chapter, we want to model how theology is done in hip-hop by using Talib Kweli's work as a case study. As we listen to his questions and answers, we will tease out his theological insights.

> *On the album Eardrum, Kweli proposes tentative answers that he claims to have heard from God in the context of the hip-hop community.*

It is important for the church to listen to hip-hop theology and culture for at least two reasons. The first reason is that maybe God is saying something to the church through the culture. God can use whatever means he wants to speak to his people. What if God is using hip-hop or popular culture to speak? If God is using hip-hop, then the church needs to listen. The second reason the church should listen is that if we hope to reach the hip-hop generation, we have to be in dialogue with its theology. The theology of the Christian church must be put in dialogue with the theology of hip-hop if a reciprocal conversion, transformation, and salvation are to occur. Let him or her who has an ear hear what Kweli is saying. As we move to track 1, we hear Kweli struggling with the issue of identity as he resists others putting on him what he should be. This is a first step in hip-hop theology: identity.

Track 1: "Everything Man"

Who is Talib Kweli? There is a lot in a name. Talib's first name is Arabian, and it means "the seeker or student." His last name is Ghanaian, meaning "of truth or knowledge." Yes, there is a lot in a name and even more in the artist/rapper/ theologian who has made his name a central part of his identity and ministry.

As the album *Eardrum* opens, we hear a poet reciting a poem about when she first heard Talib Kweli. She doesn't quite remember when that time was because it seems as though she has known him or heard him forever. Are the words of Kweli from the beginning: "In the beginning was the Word, and the Word was with God, and the Word was God" (John 1:1)? She comments on the hurricane beats and the exactness of his rhymes as he calls his followers to become thunder or creative power in their lives and to be what God has called them to be. This is the theological theme of honoring how God has created you, which is a consistent theme on this album and in much of hip-hop theology.

God is seen as a creator Spirit, and the work of creation, redemption, purpose, and destiny runs the gamut in hip-hop theology as members of the hip-hop community seek to please God and be what God has designed them to be. This principle of divine design means that those of the hip-hop generation are going to be different from those of the previous generation—different in a radical way because this is what God has created and called them to be. Not only are they going to dress differently, but their art and theological construction will also be different. They have assumed the right to develop their theological conversation outside the walls of the institutional church.

In the song "Everything Man," Kweli deals directly with the creative powers of God and what God has designed or destined a person to do. Hip-hop theology is a theology of the beat, the heartbeat. As we said earlier, hip-hop rides on the beat and internalizes itself in the devotee as the beat moves the body, heart, mind, and soul. So Kweli talks about listeners feeling the heartbeat of the song, the music, and the words as they reverberate in their eardrums. This heartbeat is also a *hard* beat that drives listeners to the mixture of the beat and the words as they work together to form an incarnational theology of who God has called them to be. Kweli claims this is destiny—his using his gift to speak a word and people hearing the word spoken as God ministers to them via hip-hop. Destiny is central in the theology of hip-hop as the hip-hop generation tries to figure out how God has called them and is leading them to walk in the valley of the shadow of death—either the inner city or the world of commercial or noncommercial hip-hop. The first verse of "Everything Man" is all about dreams, destiny, and the link to the eternal, as Kweli proclaims that the very energy for the song is "heavenly energy." The theme and theological metaphors of the song are important cues if one hopes to understand the theology in hip-hop. God is with them, in them, and using them to be and achieve what God has uniquely designed them for in this present age.

In the second verse, Kweli places himself and hip-hop in the middle of religious/theological discourse as he positions himself in the battle between God and the devil and lays claim to your spirit, your religion, your belief system. This is the root of his work. He isn't hedging on where he stands in the dialogue. He is right there in the middle, intentionally laying claim to the belief system of his listeners and informing their spirituality and religiosity. If the church hopes to engage hip-hop theology, it has to take into account how hip-hop sees itself as a cocreator with God.

This cocreative theological principle is central to hip-hop theology. God is using hip-hop to speak to people as they use their God-given gifts to write, rap, make beats, and inspire a God-conscious lifestyle for the artist and those in the hip-hop community. A God-conscious member of the hip-hop community is one who recognizes and believes that God exists but that God is bigger than any one tradition and that institutionalized religion isn't the only conduit (if it is a conduit at all) by which God communicates and makes himself known. A God-conscious member recognizes that God is active in a person's life in a type of incarnation. God acts in the real world as hip-hop lives in the moment, in the harshness of the city.

Track 2: "NY Weather Report"

In hip-hop, the urban setting is central to the creation of the culture. The city becomes the base for the creation as God enters into that space and uses artists as cocreative partners to shed light on how God manifests himself in this context. The artist takes this environment with its pros and cons and uses it as a canvas for the creation of the socio-artistic theology that he or she produces.

This cocreative theological principle is central to hip-hop theology. God is using hip-hop to speak to people as they use their God-given gifts to write, rap, make beats, and inspire a God-conscious lifestyle for the artist and those in the hip-hop community.

On the track "NY Weather Report," Kweli talks about the harsh conditions of New York City, the city of all cities. He argues that New York is a harsh environment, but if you can make it in New York, you can make it anywhere. The art of survival in the midst of harsh conditions is also key in hip-hop theology. How has God sustained people and in some cases even allowed or provided a way for them to thrive while dealing with the harsh living conditions of the city? An answer in hip-hop theology and black theology says, "God is a way out of no way."

One of the caricatures of the hip-hop artist is the artist whose album is full of vulgarity but who, upon receiving his Grammy or in his liner notes, thanks God. While this may appear to be a contradiction to the outsider, thanking God while one's album is laced with vulgarity is not a contradiction in hip-hop. It is a testament to the grace and power of God, who gave them the power to thrive in the midst of the chaos. Their work merely testifies to the chaos of the city by talking about it in real terms using the language of the streets. The language of the streets is a language that is vulgar; it is a product of the environment that rappers testify about. They can't testify in hip-hop using euphemisms. Also, hip-hop refuses to lie. It refuses to stand in the midst of the community and not talk about the struggle. Things do go wrong; people do get shot; relationships do fail. It is hard living in the city!

The journey Kweli is on in the city is navigated by the incarnational God, who is walking with him as he makes sense of the world. The journey is beginning to make sense as God gives him understanding via his third eye (which is the mind, according to Five Percenter theology).[4] He has been able to navigate his journey via blood, sweat, and tears. He has survived, and as a result, he testifies to how he made it. The problem that artists like Kweli have with "studio gangsters," or those who make up stories of struggle, is that they aren't authentic. Kweli is clear that his story is real. He has really struggled to make it in New York City. While Kweli's parents were both professors, he chose a path in life that put him in touch with the streets, struggle, and the grimier side of New York life. The things he chooses to rap about keep him out of the mainstream. He isn't selling millions, but his work is touching millions. While Kweli has resisted the label of conscious rapper, that is really what he is, and it has adversely affected his radio play. But he continues to rap about what he feels God has called him to rap about. The journey he is following has surely produced some hard times. So when he raps about struggle, he is talking about what he has come to know through experience. He condemns those whose stuff is "fake" versus those who have "really been to war." The war is survival in the city and in a capitalistic culture that profits by selling the pain of the poor. As a victim of capitalism, Kweli fights back.

Kweli screams about how the economic system of capitalism exploits the poor and how the results of this exploitation are broken families and fragile communities. "Fake" rappers who exalt the selling of drugs and violence are part of the problem. Fake rappers, according to Kweli, purport a vision of what they call success, which in essence advances a system of institutionalized oppression. Imitating what the dominant culture has produced as a paradigm of success does not help the African American community. Judgment is coming on America and on those who claim to be members of the African American community but don't work for liberation. It is in this context that God enters and speaks. As Kweli says, "It's the 3rd eye of the storm, it's the place where knowledge is born." It is in the context of struggle that one searches for revelation and God speaks and reveals a true liberating knowledge.

This is an intense contextual theology that requires God to reveal himself in the context of everyday struggle as those in the hip-hop community negotiate life's meandering journey. As Kweli says, "It is all about the journey." It is on this journey that one constantly seeks liberation. Liberation comes from God as God exposes how systems trap people, hold them down, and oppress them while they think they are being liberated and successful. Knowledge of self and knowledge of God and the ways of God are liberation. While people may still be caught in the bowels of an oppressive system, once the system has been exposed for what it is and people can begin to renegotiate their relationship with that system in a liberating manner, they are on a journey that leads to liberation. In hip-hop, salvation isn't an event but a process, a journey that leads to liberation.

Track 3: "Hostile Gospel Pt. 1 (Deliver Us)"

The cry of hip-hop theology is a cry for deliverance. As Kweli opens the third track, a chorus of voices cries, "Deliver us." This is the cry from the streets and from those who have been seduced by corporate America and have bought into the shallow American dream. As he moves to the first verse, Kweli refers to rappers as baby seals who have been government fed. The implication here is that commercial rap is supported by a system that is intent on holding African Americans down by exploiting them. This is hip-hop being reflective and self-critical. Rappers in the hip-hop industry who are going after profits and are not prophets who speak truth are a target for Kweli as he tries to make sense of the oppression African Americans continue to experience in the twenty-first century. As Kweli moves into the chorus, he asks a rhetorical question: "What the people want? Please deliver us." This cry is consistent. I would go so far as to say that those whom Kweli characterizes as government pawns and tools of oppression also want to be delivered. Who enjoys being oppressed? The problem with them is that they haven't seen the system for what it really is and they somehow believe that being pimped by the industry is freedom.

> *The cry of hip-hop theology is a cry for deliverance.*

Kweli calls the cry for deliverance the hostile gospel. This is obviously a play on the word *gospel* as used by the church culture. The hostile gospel is a cry for deliverance from a people who are fed up with institutional systems that oppress them. Kweli includes the church with those institutions that oppress others. Therefore, his gospel is not the church's gospel because he does not characterize what the institutionalized church preaches and practices as liberating. I am sure Kweli would point out that the word from the church is an oppressive word that calls for the oppressed to conform via the process of socialization to their oppressed state. The hostile gospel is the good news that people should be angry because they are tired of the oppressive state of their existence. It is up to them to fight back as they define and construct a liberating gospel that is cocreated with God via hip-hop culture.

While Kweli identifies systemic and institutionalized forms of oppression on this track, he doesn't ignore the role of personal responsibility. As the hip-hop socio-theologian takes account of the hell in the 'hood, he notes two forces at play. There are the institutional forces of racism, sexism, and classism, and then there are those personal urges that can get people in trouble. While Kweli shines a light on the institutional forces that work to hold people down, he simultaneously tells his listeners that they can get up and fight back. As he calls them to fight back and take fate into their own hands, he reveals those things they do on a personal level that work against their liberation. For example, he says to the rapper, when you allow the hip-hop industry to pimp you, you have become a partner in your own exploitation. He calls hip-hop artists not to be seduced by the American dream but instead to embrace the struggle for freedom by being both a disciple and a preacher of the hostile gospel. While those outside the African American community may wish ill on the community, God has given those inside the power to resist and to redirect their behavior. They don't have to eat, drink, or dress the way the forces that work against them tell them to. Kweli urges his followers to look deep within and find God, who wants to liberate them. There will be a constant struggle of internal and external forces, and only God—and his followers as active participants in their liberation—will overcome the power of evil.

Tracks 4 and 5: "Say Something" Featuring Jean Grae and "Country Cousins" Featuring UGK and Raheem DeVaughn

Tracks 4 and 5 complement each other as Kweli talks about the hip-hop nation as a family. It is a family that transcends borders because the words used in rap connect people. The word, as stated earlier, is that thing that carries culture and connects the hip-hop nation. The family ties that bind also lay a platform for critique and healing engagement. In "Say Something," Kweli critiques, once again, the more popular radio hip-hop. Kweli sees hip-hop as a healing balm when it is used appropriately, just as the written word when spoken works as a balm. This in-family conversation isn't shy about confronting members of the family who use hip-hop to hurt rather than to heal. This is the tension in "Say Something." Kweli and Jean Grae are engaged in a family battle with those who misuse the gift of hip-hop. This song invokes the tradition of ritual battle rap (when artists square off and duel with their lyrics) as Kweli and Jean Grae battle back and challenge those who are tearing the family down rather than building it up with the God-given gift of hip-hop. When "Say Something" and "Country Cousins" are put in dialogue, they establish hip-hop as an international family that extends across borders. Raheem DeVaughn says in the chorus of "Country Cousins," "I got cousins. . . . Like blood that's thicker than water, down dirty cross the border."

Hip-hop is bigger than its regional identities. As the theological conversation evolves, it includes all segments of hip-hop in self-reflection on how God is using hip-hop to heal and deliver. This conversation is confrontational because theological ideas bump up against one another. The way of doing theology in the context of hip-hop is dialogical and confrontational; the conversation takes the form of an ecumenical council. To those outside the hip-hop community, this theological conversation may seem to be disruptive and to produce disunity. But it actually produces unity and healing, as it brings the hip-hop community together around these theological ideas. Therefore, we can conclude that this theological conversation is a gift.

The spirit of the community is felt across borders, outside and inside concert halls, in homes, in cars, on the streets, on buses, and so on. Hip-hop transcends space and place, and the God in hip-hop is a God who unites and transcends space and place. Hip-hop doesn't invite God in; God is there. The power of God is in hip-hop as a uniting force that makes the world of hip-hop God-space.

Therefore, the world is the "church." Christians confess that God is omnipresent, but functionally they locate God and worship God in a building they call the church. Hip-hop embodies omnipresence by developing an ecclesiology that says that God isn't housed in a church. God doesn't unite hip-hop by getting people to go to a church. God unites hip-hop by transcending all borders, regions, and ethnic groups, and God unites through hip-hop. What has always amazed me and is worth mentioning again is how hip-hop transcends differences. I have never gone to a major hip-hop gathering where a major artist was performing and not been overwhelmed by how diverse the audience was in every way. On the other hand, when I go to institutionalized churches, I am always amazed at how homogenous they are.

Track 7: "Eat to Live"

When we go to track 7 on the album, we hear, "This is a ghetto prayer." Kweli says he's "prayin' for all of those who ain't got it." This song gets at the core of the theology of hip-hop as Kweli uses the voice of a little boy, whose name we come to know is Trey, crying for help. As the little boy cries for help, Kweli lets us know that his cry is a result of his hunger. He, like so many in the 'hood, is hungry. They are physically hungry and spiritually hungry. The rap of Kweli becomes one type of food, but the little boy and his family are still hungry. When Trey comes home from school, his mother asks if he had fun, but Trey's hunger drowns out his answer. He knows that once again he will go to bed hungry. His sister jokes with him, but even her jokes are overshadowed by loud growls coming from Trey's stomach. There isn't any food in the refrigerator. When Trey opens the fridge, all he sees are a couple of beers, his mother's medication. Alcohol has become her prescription for the pain of poverty.

What will become of Trey and his sister is the central question of the song. Will they wind up like their mother? Trey wants to go to the store, but he doesn't have any money, and he and his family don't have a means to generate income. He has to eat to live, and he needs strength to go to school, study, and deal with what he finds when he gets there. How does a kid survive in this world? Who hears him? Who speaks for Trey, his mother, and his sister? Who will shine a light on their struggle? Will the institutionalized church answer their cry, or will it be hip-hop?

Trey lives in a tough neighborhood and has to fight to defend himself. As Trey struggles to decide what to do, he remembers that if he walks to the store he will have to deal with both dope fiends on the corner and the kid who punched him at school. What is Trey to do? As Trey tries to choose between limited options, he remembers the voice of his grandmother, who exhorted him to pray. This is the theological tension in this song and in hip-hop theology. Where is this God to whom Trey prays? What is this God, and this God's church, doing about his suffering? He prays and prays, and it seems nothing changes. Trey finds comfort in remembering his grandma saying, "Jesus will be back any day." Trey is relieved because with nothing to eat it is getting harder to pray. He doesn't have the physical strength to pray or the spiritual will to pray.

As the song moves to the chorus, the implication of Matthew 25:31–46 comes through. The chorus raises the issue of what people actually do for those who are hungry. Kweli points out that Christians need to give to those who are in need. He is clear that we have to feed the hungry kids who have become victims of a stratified socioeconomic system that is essentially a tool of oppression. The implications of Kweli's critique are clear: we as adults are responsible for feeding the kids. This is on us. I call this theological reciprocity: we don't receive, we aren't blessed, unless we bless. If we don't feed the kids, in essence they die. We become complicit in their deaths.

As the song moves to the second verse, Kweli moves from real food to the psychological and spiritual food kids need to live. The verse begins, "My rhymes have nutritional value." This verse contains the indictment that popular culture isn't healthy for kids. (He returns to this theme over and over again.) Everything from television to music has to be scrutinized. Kids are not just fed at the table but also as they sit in front of the television or the computer screen or listen to music. Kids are being fed lies about who they are and what they can be. The implication is that leaders in our community and church must engage the larger popular culture and dialogue with that culture because Trey is in dialogue with it and does not have the tools to dissect the mixed messages.

Kweli ends the verse with an appeal that sounds a lot like John 8:32: "Lies never set you free, but the truth will. The truth still matters." This is the heart of the track: freedom. The poor are praying for freedom, and Kweli is calling people to be a part of that movement. This is about Trey, Trey's sister, Trey's mother, the dope fiends Trey passes on the way to the store; it's about the little boy who punched Trey in the face. The conditions they live in are an abomination, and the truth as it comes from hip-hop is that the church has to be a part of the liberating movement that sets the Treys of the world free. As the song ends, Kweli says, "Listen." As the song fades out, listeners hear the faint voice of Trey saying, "Is anybody gonna help us?"

Track 10: "Give 'Em Hell" Featuring Coi Mattison and Lyfe Jennings

As we journey to track 10, we hear, "We know that what we reap we sow." Theological reciprocity rears its head again. In this track, Kweli comes right at the institutionalized church. On the one hand, the theological question is, what if there isn't a heaven? On the other hand, the question is, how do we make living on earth more like heaven? The theological tension long present in black theology is present here: how do God and religion play a role in the life hereafter and the life we live now, and where should the emphasis be placed? Going to church isn't making the difference. Kweli says he has gone to all kinds of churches, but when he gets there, he doesn't hear a liberating word but rather the weekly gossip. The institutionalized church has lost its relevance with regard to being a liberating agent that speaks to the 'hood.

Kweli brings up an old argument that Mark Chapman raised in his book *Christianity on Trial: African-American Religious Thought before and after Black Power*. Chapman says, "The African American community *must* continue to critique manifestations of Christianity from inside and outside the church walls if the black institutional church is to be an effective witness to the liberating gospel of Jesus Christ."[5] Kweli critiques the black institutionalized church from outside the walls of the church. He calls the church out while simultaneously claiming that maybe the church is actually outside the church. In the first verse, Kweli talks about going to church every Sunday, dressed up, only to hear gossip. Not only is he hearing gossip, but he also questions the very word that is preached from the pulpit. Kweli raises the central question of his critique: is the word preached from the pulpit the Word?

Just as Kweli called rappers out, he now calls preachers out. This is the core liberating edge in hip-hop theology. It is a theology that demands the prophetic to be spoken and lived.

For Kweli, it isn't about a specific denomination or branch of the church; they all appear equally irrelevant and ineffective. According to Kweli, he can't see a difference in the Baptist or the Catholic Church, or any other denomination for that matter. They are all preaching the same message that coincides with and supports the oppressive structures that Kweli is speaking against. The church as an institution has trapped the masses and has become a part of the oppressive force in the 'hood. The worth of the word of ecclesiastical authorities is held in question because their words and theology endorse and participate in an oppressive system. Just as Kweli called rappers out, he now calls preachers out. This is the core liberating edge in hip-hop theology. It is a theology that demands the prophetic to be spoken and lived. Hip-hop theology reaches back to the likes of James Cone and is the prophetic voice that Cone was in the late 1960s and early 1970s.

Kweli asks directly whether the word coming from the pulpit is anything of liberating substance. Is the word of one who calls himself or herself pastor/ preacher worth more than the word of anyone who is in touch with God? If we are all God's children, then we all hear from God and have a divine connection to speak to God and on behalf of God. What Christians might call the priesthood of all believers is taken to another extreme in this track. Kweli makes the point, if we are made in the image of God, then we have to look like God, hear from

God, and speak on behalf of God. In the African American church, the image of God that is portrayed is no more than the old missionary God, a white god, or worse, a god of capitalism. Kweli pushes the envelope here and proclaims that African Americans are the very image of God. God has to look like them. If people don't look like their God, Kweli suggests that they are religious bastards. African Americans aren't bastards. Members of the hip-hop nation aren't bastards. God looks like them. The very image of God is transformed into hip-hop as God becomes hip-hop. Hip-hop followers refused to allow an institutional church to disown them. God owns them, God created them in his image, and God is using them to get his Word out to those of the hip-hop family who don't participate in institutionalized forms of religion.

Hip-hop theology critiques the coalescing of religion with state and political power, in which religion then becomes a tool of state oppression. Kweli makes this point plain as he expounds on King James and his use of religion. Kweli goes on to say that institutionalized, politicized religion creates division. Hip-hop theology is extremely tolerant and sees syncretism and pluralism as central components of religious life. Hip-hop theology has room for various religious traditions and merges those belief systems into a theological tapestry that looks more like a remix or a quilt than a denominational belief statement that defines who is in or out, right or wrong.

The institutional church seeks to control theological conversation, and this defies the role of the divine as understood in hip-hop theology. For hip-hop, the divine principles of the theological conversation are openness, inclusion, and acceptance of differences. According to Kweli, the don'ts of religion, the Ten Commandments, the thou-shalt-nots, are not what is needed. What is needed are the do's. Kweli wants to turn the theological negatives into positives. How should theology tell people what to do rather than what not to do? As people deal with the struggles they face, a to-do list should guide them. Kweli says, "I've dealt with my base self, I controlled my many urges." In hip-hop, the Spirit of God is a power within that guides people, gives them the ability to control themselves, and keeps them from doing wrong. It isn't remembering the catechism that makes the difference; it's God living within that makes the difference.

The heaven-and-hell debate drives the song—the premise being that hell is right here on earth. Do you know hell? Do you know what it feels like and looks like? Kweli says, "If you ever walked through any ghetto then you know it well." Living in the ghetto is hell. Hip-hop theology doesn't fully embrace the afterlife the way traditional Christians might believe in heaven and hell. They are more convinced that hell is here on earth. Their theology is rooted in the reality of today without holding on to the promise of an afterlife in heaven. In many ways, the advancing of a theology that pushes people to believe in heaven and the afterlife is seen as a way to distract those who are living in hell or producing conditions that create and sustain the pain of the poor from changing the conditions. It relieves them of the responsibility to make this life better. As the chorus in the song continues to ask, "If we don't get to heaven it's hell, we all livin' in hell." So if there isn't any heaven, we have really been duped. What we can and do believe and know through experience is that we are living in hell. So we have to commit to making this hell into heaven and fighting to make living conditions on earth better. These living conditions are about more than money and wealth. They are about justice, equality, and freedom. A hip-hop theology of liberation is what informs what living on earth should look like, and it is not the capitalist dream that so many have bought into.

The God of hip-hop is a God who is found inside those who follow this God. This is the incarnational principle amplified. God isn't manifested via a preacher preaching, a choir singing, or a deacon praying. God makes himself known in the life of the follower/believer. This doesn't completely count the institutionalized church out, but it does open the doors of the institutionalized church. Hip-hop theology sees the omnipresence of God in a real incarnational way that radicalizes how the indwelling of God's presence is made manifest.

Kweli sees his poetry as divine. What he means is that the very words he is rapping in his songs are divine and that God is ministering through him. Kweli and many in hip-hop would argue that God skipped past the church and came to them. God doesn't need the church. God can come to whomever God wants to, and no body or institution has to ordain them, train them, or police them. This is a radical religious freedom, and it is one of the ways hip-hop theology pushes the theological conversation from the church to the streets to the concert hall to the individual. Hip-hop has a direct line to God, which challenges the church to call what hip-hop does heretical or blasphemous. Hip-hop pushes back and labels the church heretical.

Track 19: "Hostile Gospel Pt. 2 (Deliver Me)" Featuring Sizzla

On track 19, Kweli continues his hostile gospel. Part 2 of the hostile gospel resurrects the cry for deliverance, actual deliverance. Kweli resets the struggle of those in the inner city in dialogue with hip-hop and God. When I say "actual deliverance," I mean that Kweli isn't calling for a prayer or a laying on of hands with the promise of God showing up. Rather, he is calling for action. He says he would rather die on his feet before he would live on his knees. The interesting thing here is that he is addressing God. He isn't addressing the institutional church. He isn't talking to preachers, priests, or imams. He is talking to God. Kweli, the theologian of hip-hop, is coming straight at God and calling on God to act. He wants deliverance from the evil that surrounds him, and he wants deliverance for those who are struggling against a system that is intent on holding them down. It is as if Kweli is revisiting William Jones's old argument, "Is God a white racist?" God is now on the witness stand. Kweli is calling out to God, "God, deliver us from evil!"

The hip-hop theologian rails against systems of oppression, gods of oppression. Capitalism, while glorified on one hand as a source of liberation, is seen as a tool of oppression on the other. Hip-hop theologians are caught, like all theologians, as they try to address the economic system they find themselves victims of. The system, capitalism, has locked brothers and sisters into a cycle of minimum wage—a wage that can barely keep them housed and fed. While they work, what appears to be a way to freedom is actually reformed slavery. This is the dual nature of capitalism: it presents itself as a way out, but it is really a way to keep one in. Even if one achieves what would be considered financial wealth, he or she is still a slave to the system. The people Kweli is speaking for and to are those who are held in a system that makes them slaves. The employment system is not meant for freedom. As people seek to become the consumers that they are shaped to be, they become even more enslaved to the things they buy, which in turn own them. They are owned as they attempt to own because credit brings debt, which in turn enslaves. The hard worker turned consumer trying to be a provider is duped in the process. There is a circular nature to the oppressive system, and the hip-hop theologian calls to God for deliverance.

The chorus in the song talks about the evil around us and the temptation this evil brings. In hip-hop theology, evil and the devil are real. Kweli is talking about real evil that results in ruined lives. Drugs, gangs, and sexually transmitted diseases are all manifestations of the evil that both tempts and kills those of the hip-hop nation. On the one hand, Kweli says hip-hop is a part of this world and at times contributes to the evil via its appeal to lead a sinful life. On the other hand, Kweli calls for hip-hop not to do that, to be an "underground railroad" to freedom. In this context, the hip-hop theologian includes hip-hop in his critique as being party to the evil in the 'hood. At the same time, he offers options for hip-hop not to be a part of the problem. Kweli talks about how evil is in people and how by their own evil desires, as they attempt to sedate themselves in the harsh world they live in, they resort to sin or evil as a comfort, but in the end it is a killer. He mentions the man who drinks whiskey straight because he can't stand to see his child hungry and he is unable to find employment to feed the child. This example takes us back to that classic hit "The Message." The pain of not being able to provide for a family is a serious issue that hip-hop addresses; it addresses the systemic economic issues that work against liberation. The hip-hop theologian has a macro approach to understanding the problem of pain and evil in the 'hood that is linked to survival and liberation.

Track 20: "The Nature" Featuring Justin Timberlake

As Kweli closes out this album, he sends a prophetic warning by talking about the direction society is going. It is going in a dangerous direction. Families are being destroyed, poverty is running rampant, and intimate relationships are a thing of the past. In this harsh world, Kweli asks, "Who does God go through?"

Hip-hop theologians challenge all boundaries of traditional theological categories and ways of doing theology. The parameters are removed in a no-limits theological conversation. Everything is on the table.

His answer is that God uses prophets. The prophets of the day are calling people to get back to what really matters. To get back to what really matters, people have to be true to that still, small voice inside that is calling them not only to speak truth but also to seek truth. What really matters are relationships, noticing one another, loving one's family, and making the world a more just place to live.

What will get people back to what really matters is faith. Faith is grown and developed as people get through what they go through. God is the object of one's faith, but this faith is strengthened not by being a part of a "faith community" in the traditional sense or practicing religion as outlined by the institutionalized church. Rather, faith is built up by the Spirit-led activities of everyday life. As people live their lives, go through struggles, survive, experience times of love, family, and joy, their faith grows. As a hip-hop theologian, Kweli is saying that life as lived in the real world with real people is a type of church. Ecclesiology in this context comes outside the institutionalized church and becomes life. Lived experience becomes where people encounter God and live a godly life. The theological theme that runs through this final track is that God is bigger than a church. Kweli, like hip-hop, has taken God to the world and set God free.

Bonus Track: The Essence of Hip-Hop Theology

Hip-hop theologians challenge all boundaries of traditional theological categories and ways of doing theology. The parameters are removed in a no-limits theological conversation. Everything is on the table. They aren't looking for the church or the seminary to confirm them, anoint them, or agree with them. They are asking hard questions to a real God in a real world. The theological canvas is not the hallowed halls of the seminary or the cozy Bible study in the church basement; their theological canvas is the harsh lived reality of the city. If pressed to make some concluding observations regarding the foundation of hip-hop theology, I would suggest the following eight central themes:

1. Hip-hop theology is an incarnational theology that sees God as cocreating in hip-hop.

2. Hip-hop theology is a contextual theology in which theological reflection addresses the harsh living conditions of the inner city in a capitalistic environment.
3. Hip-hop theology embraces the theological principle of reaping and sowing, or what I like to call theological reciprocity, meaning, you get what you give, and you are called to give and do good.
4. The hostile gospel recognizes that evil is real and is imposed both from without and from within. Hip-hop theology is centered on deliverance from this evil as it manifests itself in the community.
5. Hip-hop theologians do theology in the context of hip-hop culture, and this theology is dialogical and confrontational. It takes the form of an ecumenical council that calls for healing within the hip-hop community. God acts in the context of these theological conversations from track to track. The music serves as a God-ordained healing agent.
6. Hip-hop theology is rooted in the story of Matthew 25:31–46, where Christ comes to judge between the sheep and the goats. The sheep in the story meet people's everyday needs. Hip-hop theology can be considered a sheep theology; it is about meeting people where their hurt is and offering tangible help that makes an immediate and real difference.
7. The hip-hop theologian doesn't need a word from an appointed representative of the institutionalized church. God is a God of grace and speaks to all. We all are prophets and prophetesses, preachers, priests and priestesses. Institutionalized religion is a political tool used to divide and conquer. Hip-hop has no part in the institution but rather seeks God by looking inside a person, where God resides and empowers.
8. Hip-hop is the image of God to the extent that God is reflected in hip-hop culture.

Getting in Touch with Hip-Hop

Kweli, Talib. *Eardrum*. Blacksmith/Warner Bros., 2007.

7

the miseducation of lauryn hill

A Socio-Theological Critique of Hip-Hop

So What Now?

This final chapter brings us to the point of critiquing hip-hop. At times I feel as though I don't need to engage in a critique of hip-hop because that appears to be the order of the day. The critics are too numerous to cite. The critiques of hip-hop are varied and at times substantive. But in the end, critique is needed and warranted and must be engaged in. In this chapter, I hope to push us all to think about new questions that will lead to a critique and engagement of hip-hop at a different level. Ranting about the obvious misogyny, sexism, violence, and materialism of hip-hop, as much as they need to be critiqued, is too easy.

We need to ask deeper questions about how the hip-hop industry has used hip-hop culture to demonize African American art, to profit from the poverty in inner-city America, to use the classic Jezebel and gangsta images to further criminalize and demonize the black body. How has the hip-hop industry used hip-hop culture to lower the self-esteem of African American women and men? Have the hip-hop industry and hip-hop culture become so blurred or intertwined that we cannot untangle them? Is this even a profitable conversation? What are the long-term socioeconomic and psychological effects of the video forms of hip-hop? What are the images that they promote, portray, and condone doing to the future of African Americans in how they see themselves and how others see them?

115

How has the hip-hop industry used hip-hop culture to lower the self-esteem of African American women and men? Have the hip-hop industry and hip-hop culture become so blurred or intertwined that we cannot untangle them?

This conversation will take place in a Barack Obama America—an America that now says a black man can become president. The lack of understanding of how racism, classism, and sexism intersect to form a web of oppression in America will increase. In this Obama America, pundits are already talking about a postracial America. Contrary to popular rhetoric, however, classism, sexism, and racism are very much alive.

If a black man can be president, what does that say about the great number of African Americans oppressed by a web of racism, classism, and sexism? Will hip-hop become the tool that is used in some form or fashion in American culture to blame African Americans for the poverty in which the majority of black people live? Will hip-hop be used to divide the "good" blacks from the "bad" blacks? Will America chime in with Bill Cosby and say, "Come on, people"? How will hip-hop be a part of the larger cultural debate around race and class? These are the types of questions that should fuel a more robust critical engagement of hip-hop. Unfortunately, this level of engagement lies beyond the scope of this book. Instead, I will provide a specific, narrower critique.

Track 1: Do You See What I Hear?

The critique of hip-hop in this chapter will use a socio-theological lens. I will introduce a critical engagement that is rooted in a healthy, balanced feminism in conversation with the Bible. As much as God may be working in hip-hop culture, there are some things in hip-hop that I am sure God doesn't condone. As we embark on this more focused and nuanced critical engagement—this socio-theological critique of hip-hop—I put Lauryn Hill in dialogue with the woman at the well (John 4:1–30).

This biblical story shows a woman critiquing the social and theological ethics of the day as she says to Jesus, "'You are a Jew and I am a Samaritan woman. How can you ask me for a drink?' (For Jews do not associate with Samaritans)" (John 4:9). In this exchange, the Samaritan woman is exegeting the culture and calling Jesus and his band to task for their ethnic and religious segregationist and sectarian practices. She is saying something about the way women are treated. She is saying something about the theological roots of Judaism. She is talking out of her pain and hurt that result from the exclusion and oppression of women in this culture. This Samaritan woman could be a hip-hop feminist because hip-hop also displays oppressive and segregationist tendencies as it relates to women.

This final chapter seeks a sustained critical conversation that will help hip-hop rather than condemn the art or the culture. This sustained critical conversation is inspired by what Michael Dyson calls "ethical patience." We have been patient and have looked at the upside of hip-hop; now we move to a more critical engagement as we use the Bible and the moral compass of hip-hop to critique a culture that is riddled with problems of materialism, sexism, and misogyny. These problems are exacerbated by the conflicted identity of hip-hop culture versus the hip-hop industry.

Lauryn Hill: the miseducated educates us

Ruff House Records/Photofest

The Miseducation of Lauryn Hill will lead us in this conversation. The thesis of this album will inform our conversation as we try to identify the elements of hip-hop that could potentially destroy the value of this God-given art. If hip-hop culture were to look into the mirror of the larger dominant culture and ask, are we really that different, what would it find? Is it too simplistic to reduce hip-hop culture to a reflection of American culture? Should hip-hop culture be singled out as the variable that is causing the violence, decay, sexism, and so forth that we see in America? These questions place our critique of hip-hop in the context of the larger American culture of which it is a part. In raising these questions, I am not dodging the issues and concerns surrounding hip-hop and the hip-hop industry. I am simply trying to contextualize the critique. A critique of hip-hop can't forget that hip-hop culture is a product of American culture. Hip-hop is as Americana as apple pie, baseball, and NASCAR. This critique is not a blame game. Hip-hop can't be blamed for all things bad in America or the African American community. This critique of hip-hop aims to help those involved in hip-hop to be more reflective and self-critical as well as to raise questions that move us to think deeply about hip-hop so as not to celebrate it without also critiquing it. As my momma would say, "There is always room for critique."

Track 2: Who Dat Talkin' 'Bout Hip-Hop?

I want to position this critique of hip-hop inside hip-hop culture. This critique is an insider's take. A critique of hip-hop from inside hip-hop has a certain authenticity because it is rooted in love. Erykah Badu spoke for many devotees when she proclaimed that hip-hop was the love of her life.[1] Many critiques of hip-hop are missing the love element. This critical engagement, which is inspired by love, involves hip-hop, the biblical voice, and the voice of Gil Scott-Heron, one of the founders of rap and to some extent hip-hop culture. Scott-Heron and his "Message to the Messengers"—or hip-hop artists—is something that must be heard. He exposes the contradictions that are a part of hip-hop culture that this critique will confront. Scott-Heron called this generation out when he exposed the contradictions in calling a woman queen on one track and then calling her out of her name on the next track by referring to women in a derogatory manner. Artists can't have it both ways.[2]

Scott-Heron calls for consistency in the culture. The B-word isn't a term of affection or endearment. It is a derogatory characterization of women, and its use by the hip-hop culture needs to be dealt with. Hip-hop lyrics about women send mixed messages about how women are to be treated and included in the culture. This sexism in the lyrics, culture, and ethos of hip-hop needs to be exorcised. Hip-hop artists can't be let off the hook. The culture is riddled with an abusive sexist ideology that has to be corrected. When Lauryn Hill cries about her miseducation, one of the issues she is referring to is the way she and her sisters have been abused in their relationships with men and in hip-hop culture.

Track 3: The Miseducation of Hip-Hop: Introducing a Feminist Critique

It is appropriate to start this insider's critique with Lauryn Hill because, unlike many female hip-hop artists, she had the best of both worlds. She was down with a crew, the Fugees, and successfully transitioned to become a bona fide hip-hop star on her own. Her relationships with the Fugees, men, and the record business fuel her critique as she openly deals with the sexist ideology and misogyny in hip-hop culture.

What do we mean when we label Lauryn Hill a hip-hop feminist? Gwendolyn Pough offers this definition: "A hip-hop feminist is more than someone who likes and listens to rap music and feels conflicted about it. A hip-hop feminist is someone who is immersed in hip-hop culture and experiences hip-hop as a way of life. Hip-hop as a culture, in turn, influences his or her worldview or approach to life."[3] When you listen to Lauryn Hill, you hear a person who is thoroughly hip-hop while not defined by the negative influences of hip-hop culture. Hip-hop for Hill is a way of life but not the totality of her life. She is hip-hop while not letting hip-hop confine her. Hip-hop culture definitely influences Hill's worldview, but she also talks back to hip-hop as an active agent who is simultaneously shaping hip-hop. Hill asserts her womanhood and critiques the culture from within the culture when she stands up and speaks about the sexist, capitalistic pulls of the hip-hop industry. Her experience of being a woman who is hip-hop inform her critique. The relationships she has enjoyed and endured in the hip-hop culture and industry are evident in her artistic production.

When you listen to Lauryn Hill, you hear a person who is thoroughly hip-hop while not defined by the negative influences of hip-hop culture. Hip-hop for Hill is a way of life but not the totality of her life.

As a hip-hop feminist, Hill sees herself and her peers as shapers of hip-hop culture. They can stand up against the exploitive features of the culture. As Pough extends her definition of a hip-hop feminist, the role of Hill and her peers becomes more evident:

[Hip-hop feminists] hold themselves and their peers responsible for effecting change in the present and future by encouraging people to recognize and combat their own complicity and complacency. In terms of rap music and hip-hop culture, they want to find ways to move beyond counting the amount of times a particular rapper says the word "bitch" or "ho," to focus on what they consider to be larger issues and concerns. For example, they also want to begin to complicate understandings of women's complicity in the objectification of women especially as it pertains to video-hos.[4]

Hill as a hip-hop feminist continues to challenge hip-hop to be honest with itself by raising the bigger issues of the exploitation of a culture and a people. Hip-hop can't hide behind the veil of "keeping it real" or "being the 'hood's CNN." Hip-hop must confront the question, how are we a part of the problems of the city? How is hip-hop culture complicit in creating an environment of sexism, misogyny, and capitalistic greed? Hill also brings women in hip-hop to task as she asks, how are we participating in the assault on the female image by being used as a pawn in the acts that result in degrading images of African American women?

Track 4: Lost One with Lost Souls: Is Hip-Hop Selling Soul or Has Hip-Hop *Souled* Out?

What good is it for a man to gain the whole world, yet forfeit his soul? (Mark 8:36)

The first track of *The Miseducation of Lauryn Hill* goes right to the heart of the issue: has hip-hop *souled* out or sold out? Hip-hop has grown up to become a commercial success, and as a result, what has happened to hip-hop? Hill's critique does not come from a purist who hasn't been commercially successful. When she released *The Miseducation of Lauryn Hill*, she had seen success on the small screen and the big screen. She had also had a major release with the Fugees. This isn't a critique of a has-been or a wannabe. She has made it. And as she reflects on what she has gleaned from this experience, she raises some serious questions about hip-hop and her relationship with hip-hop.

Her first major question confronts the cash cow that hip-hop culture has become for American capitalism. What has it cost hip-hop to be sold and bought by the highest bidder? Has cultural and artistic integrity been sacrificed on the altar of profits? If so, has hip-hop compromised its potential of being prophetic, liberating, and healing? While I extol the redemptive principle of hip-hop and the possibility of God's presence in the culture, the issues Hill raises can't be dismissed. As she says in "Lost One," when money entered the picture of hip-hop, the liberation factor was lost. By being a cash cow for capitalistic gain, does hip-hop imprison the art, the artist, and its followers?

The question then becomes, is hip-hop being a liberating agent for women, especially women of color, or for other oppressed groups? Moreover, is hip-hop a liberating agent for men of color who pattern their sexist ways on the dominant American culture and, like the dominant culture, oppress women and espouse misogynistic images and lifestyles? As Hill continues her opening anthem and moves to the chorus, she is clear that some hip-hop artists are caught up in the game of the hip-hop industry, but the industry will not get her to buy in or sell out. Hill calls all of us to rebel against the corruption of the liberating art of hip-hop perpetrated by the hip-hop industry. On what became one of the top-selling and most decorated hip-hop albums, she refuses to buy in. It is like the question Patricia Hill Collins raises: "Is buying in selling out?"[5] Collins proclaims that the question is as important as the answer. We must constantly ask ourselves, have we bought into a system that promises what it isn't designed to deliver?

The record/entertainment industry isn't designed to set people free. Hill proclaimed, at the peak of her "success," that she would not get caught in this trap. The truth in her cry was confirmed in her follow-up album, *MTV Unplugged 2.0*, as she openly rebelled against the hip-hop industry.[6] Some said she had lost her mind, but when you listen intently to *The Miseducation of Lauryn Hill*, you should sense what was to come next in *Unplugged 2.0*. Hill was a hip-hop feminist in the truest sense, and her commitment to a hip-hop feminist critique would mature as she matured. Not only was she calling the culture and the industry to task, but she was also taking a stand against the exploitive nature of the business by turning away from the business. She desperately tried to keep hip-hop free from the constraints of the hip-hop industry so that it could serve as an agent of liberation for so many others.

Hill came to the simple conclusion early in her career that the selling of one's soul for profit is unhealthy. In the end, who wins? No one wins. The passage from Mark 8:36 is instructive here. What has hip-hop or the African American community or America at large gained by selling its soul (soul music)? Cee Lo Green says, "Whether you're selling a dream, selling a scheme, or playing a role; like it or not we're selling soul."[7]

How do we participate in undermining the prophetic potential of hip-hop by the albums we buy, the videos we watch, the artists we support? Is there a difference in buying a Lil Wayne album versus a Talib Kweli album, or a Trina album versus a Meshell Ndegeocello album? As we put the spotlight on hip-hop, it reflects on all of us and our connection with hip-hop and exploitive systems as a whole. The question at hand is this: has hip-hop been a profit-maker instead of a prophet-maker? The Luke passage that has served as the foundation of black theology must be put in conversation with the Mark 8:36 passage:

> The scroll of the prophet Isaiah was handed to him. Unrolling it, he found the place where it is written:
>
> "The Spirit of the Lord is upon me,
>   because he has anointed me
>   to preach good news to the poor.
> He has sent me to proclaim freedom for the prisoners
>   and recovery of sight for the blind,
> to release the oppressed,
>   to proclaim the year of the Lord's favor." (Luke 4:17–19)

For hip-hop to be truly liberating, it has to come to terms with the price the culture has paid for selling its soul. If the culture has compromised its freedom message for a corporately packaged message, then hip-hop and the hip-hop generation are in trouble. The word from Luke 4:17–19 speaks to hip-hop and calls on hip-hop to embrace the liberating message of Jesus and black theology. As Will Coleman says, "Black theology is a theology of witness and liberation."[8] The question that returns to hip-hop is, are you being a witness that liberates? A witness that wallows in the pain of oppression or contributes to the oppression of a people is not liberating. Hip-hop culture must see Luke 4:17–19 as a corrective that can inform its future liberating work. Does hip-hop need a savior? I hear Lecrae saying, "Here am I, send me!"

On track 6 of *Miseducation*, Hill raises the question of the purpose and role of hip-hop in terms of liberation. Music is supposed to inspire, cries Hill in the chorus. She suggests that the purpose of music and hip-hop culture is to inspire and uplift people. The concept of uplifting is central to the historic freedom struggles of the African American community. Hill employs the concept of uplifting to suggest that if music and hip-hop culture were doing what they are supposed to do, then people would be doing better than they are; the African American community would be better off than it is.

How do we participate in undermining the prophetic potential of hip-hop by the albums we buy, the videos we watch, the artists we support? Is there a difference in buying a Lil Wayne album versus a Talib Kweli album, or a Trina album versus a Meshell Ndegeocello album?

If the people who should be leading the freedom movement have been seduced by a system of oppression, who is to lead the freedom struggle? Hill points to the liberating work of Christ, saying that stardom should not be the goal of hip-hop artists. Their goal should be to be like Christ. If the goal is to be like Christ, then Luke 4:17–19 becomes the central text for hip-hop along with John 3:16–17. Jesus was not sent to condemn the world but to save it. Hip-hop is not sent to condemn the culture but to save hip-hop culture from the hip-hop industry. How can hip-hop save the culture from the abuses of the hip-hop industry and consumerism?

As the song progresses, Hill suggests that hip-hop has tasted a drug of money, sex, and fame, and the culture is now hooked on this drug, which is killing the artist, the culture, and the people. There is no getting around the fact that the hip-hop industry has used hip-hop culture to glorify materialism, consumerism, sexism, and misogyny. The artists who bought into the myth of success are now empty. When the industry is through using certain artists, it throws them away. They are cast aside along with their catalog. Then the next "superstar" is anointed, not to liberate but to contribute to the assault on the African American body, image, and culture. What has this industry cost the artist, the art, the culture, and the people?

Hill agrees that every cause has an effect. What is the cause and effect between what is portrayed in hip-hop culture and what we see happening in the streets of the cities around the globe and especially in the African American communities, Latino communities, and suburbs where white kids have come to love hip-hop?[9] How much is hip-hop to blame? While some want to blame hip-hop for all the ills of the African American community, and on the other extreme, some want to say hip-hop bears none of the blame, the truth is somewhere in between. Hip-hop is contributing to the fallout. Racism, sexism, and institutionalized systems of oppression can't be discounted as roots of the problem, but hip-hop can't be excused from watering the root that produces this "strange fruit."[10] To disentangle the two, the root and the fruit, is a difficult task, but systems of oppression and how hip-hop culture contributes to the promotion of oppressive states are worthy of discussion. There is blood on the hands of hip-hop culture as manifested and promoted through the hip-hop industry.

Track 5: Forgive Them, Father: Forgiveness and Hip-Hop

Jesus said, "Father, forgive them, for they do not know what they are doing." (Luke 23:34)

Miseducation's "Forgive Them Father" introduces us to forgiveness in hip-hop. This is an appropriate topic as we critique hip-hop. On the one hand, most major artists are young adults or teenagers. I wonder how they are going to reflect on what they did in their early years once they mature. On the other hand, executives in the hip-hop industry are full-grown adults, and they know what they are doing. When it comes to forgiving these two broadly defined populations—young artists and industry executives—it doesn't mean they are given a pass. What it means is that we have to bring the biblical concept of forgiveness to the critique. Forgiveness has to be a part of the critique because only a foundation of love will lead to repentance and reconciliation. Critique and confrontation that do not lead to repentance and reconciliation do not achieve the desired end.

When Hill suggests in the song "Forgive Them Father" that they don't know what they are doing, I want to include both groups: the executives and others in the industry along with the young artists. There is no way that hip-hop can know its full power and impact, positively or negatively, on the larger culture. As much as the dollars and cents tell us something about the power and influence of hip-hop, it is still difficult to draw a causal line between hip-hop and the ills of our society. A line is present—or should we say lines are present—but it is difficult to connect hip-hop to this or that specific effect. Hip-hop obviously influences a great deal, but Hill raises the question, do they really know what they are doing? Hill suggests that they are confused and lost in a sea of greed.

> *Hill points to the liberating work of Christ, saying that stardom should not be the goal of hip-hop artists. Their goal should be to be like Christ.*

The list of those who have focused on "getting theirs" in terms of money, wealth, and fame is too numerous to name, Hill suggests. The system has caught them and bought them, and instead of judging them, Hill prays for them. Hill points to Luke 23:34, where Jesus says, "Father, forgive them, for they do not know what they are doing."

Two other men, both criminals, were also led out with him to be executed. When they came to the place called The Skull, there they crucified him, along with the criminals—one on his right, the other on his left. Jesus said, "Father, forgive them, for they do not know what they are doing." And they divided up his clothes by casting lots.

The people stood watching, and the rulers even sneered at him. They said, "He saved others; let him save himself if he is the Christ of God, the Chosen One."

The soldiers also came up and mocked him. They offered him wine vinegar and said, "If you are the king of the Jews, save yourself."

There was a written notice above him, which read: THIS IS THE KING OF THE JEWS.

One of the criminals who hung there hurled insults at him: "Aren't you the Christ? Save yourself and us!"

But the other criminal rebuked him. "Don't you fear God," he said, "since you are under the same sentence? We are punished justly, for we are getting what our deeds deserve. But this man has done nothing wrong."

Then he said, "Jesus, remember me when you come into your kingdom."

Jesus answered him, "I tell you the truth, today you will be with me in paradise." (Luke 23:32–43)

In this passage, the soldiers divide Jesus's clothes. They are probably going to sell these garments at a later date to one of Jesus's followers. The soldiers mock Jesus as the political system of the day has its way with Jesus and crucifies him on a cross between two thieves. Ironically, the political and religious leaders of that day recognize who Jesus is while simultaneously trying to contain his power and deny his divinity. In essence, they recognize his power and try to kill his power. Placing him between two thieves was a way of denying his divinity. Yet, while Jesus is on a hill between two thieves, his Father recognizes him and so do the true followers of Jesus.

Hip-hop too is between two thieves. The two thieves are the corporate culture and those who have stolen the soul of a community by assaulting the self-worth and identity of a people. The hip-hop industry has effectively pimped or used hip-hop culture, and many of the participants in the industry are from the communities that birthed and support the culture. The ironic twist is that, as with the Jesus story, there is still saving power in hip-hop. Hill is saying to the thieves, "Wake up. Look at what is between you. It is hip-hop; hip-hop is on the cross."

Can we save hip-hop, or can hip-hop save us? To get at the answer to this question, we must return to forgiveness. Forgiveness is tied up with confession and repentance. The hip-hop industry must both confess and repent of its ways. What is hip-hop—the industry and the culture—called to be by God? This question is one hip-hop has to answer. The Cross Movement is a group of holy hip-hop artists who are trying to answer the question of God's purpose for hip-hop, and they are doing it by using hip-hop for the glory of God and to seek and save that which is lost.

Back to the Jesus story. The twist in the Jesus story is that during the ultimate sacrifice and pain, Jesus forgives. While one thief mocks Jesus and the other recognizes that he is the Son of God, Jesus forgives all in the same moment as he becomes the atoning sacrifice for our sin. Jesus utters words of forgiveness and welcomes the thief into the kingdom.

This is where Hill sits and where many hip-hop feminists like myself sit. We are in the middle of the hill with the thieves, and we are trying to forgive. If the church doesn't approach hip-hop the way Jesus approached the cross and the thieves, how can there be hope for salvation? How can we save what we don't love? How can we save what we aren't willing to forgive? What reigned supreme on that hill where Jesus was crucified was the love of God. To engage hip-hop and save the hip-hop generation, the ethic of love must be our guide. Hill holds hip-hop accountable for its complicity in the crime, but the principles of forgiveness, restoration, reconciliation, redemption, and love guide her. Hip-hop has been miseducated, abused, and misused. Hip-hop is a sheep in the midst of wolves. According to Hill, hip-hop has been misused by the hip-hop industry, and this misuse and abuse has resulted in hip-hop lying to itself, and a critique of hip-hop and the hip-hop industry, in love, exposes the lie. The men and women of the hip-hop industry who claim to love hip-hop and the hip-hop generation are promoting and selling death to a people who are looking for life.

> *If the church doesn't approach hip-hop the way Jesus approached the cross and the thieves, how can there be hope for salvation? How can we save what we don't love?*

Track 6: Correcting the Miseducation in Hip-Hop and of the Hip-Hop Generations: Between Motown and Def Jam

For God so loved the world that he gave his one and only Son, that whoever believes in him shall not perish but have eternal life. For God did not send his Son into the world to condemn the world, but to save the world through him. (John 3:16–17)

I am always moved by John 3:16–17. What moves me is that God sends his son to save a world that is worthy of condemnation. The love of God is so powerful that instead of condemning what should have been condemned, God sends his Son to save it. Did God see something in the world that was worth redeeming? Did God care for his creation so much that he wasn't willing to condemn it? This text pushes us to think about how to deal with a culture or an art that some may want to condemn. The question comes back to us: how would God act? We know one possible answer based on how God has already acted. God so loved the world that God sent his son to save the world! If, as Hill suggests, hip-hop has been miseducated, the love of God as manifested through the act of salvation calls us to go, love, and teach hip-hop and correct the miseducation.

The title says it all—or does it? *The Miseducation of Lauryn Hill*. We also have to ask a final question, from the title cut: what does she mean by *miseducation*? Maybe she is referring to the work of the late Carter G. Woodson, the historian of African American history, and his classic text, *The Miseducation of the Negro*. Woodson said, "When you control a man's thinking you do not have to worry about his actions. You do not have to tell him not to stand here or go yonder. He will find his 'proper place' and will stay in it. You do not need to send him to the back door. He will go without being told. In fact, if there is no back door, he will cut one for his special benefit. His education makes it necessary."[11]

On the final track, Hill reflects on what the hip-hop industry has done to her and the minds of hip-hop's followers. The hip-hop industry has tried to push her into a form it wants her and hip-hop to be, and she is actively resisting that "squeeze." The past glory days of hip-hop—as she says, "being a ghetto superstar"—are long gone. Hill is now in the throes of the hip-hop industry, and she wonders what has happened to hip-hop culture. Hill cries out that when she tries to be something that the industry wants her to be, it stifles her creativity. She then strikes back in the chorus by proclaiming that the answer lies within her. She has to make up her mind what she will be as God leads her in defining her destiny.

In essence, Hill is producing what Patricia Hill Collins calls "oppositional knowledge." "For Black feminist thought, remaining oppositional involves challenging the constructs, paradigms, and epistemologies of bodies of knowledge that have more power, authority, and/or legitimacy than Black feminist thought."[12] In the context of hip-hop culture, the male voices and patriarchy have been the order of the day. For Hill to break away from the Fugees, a male-dominated group, and do her own thing was a major step. She realized that she had power and a voice. Her critique of the sexism and patriarchy in the culture goes one step further in defining who she is. She develops oppositional knowledge as she shares her brand of feminist thought and ways of knowing. "For Black feminist thought, oppositionality represents less of an achieved state of being than a state of becoming."[13] On this album, Hill is becoming Hill the thinker, the liberator, the self God created her to be as she navigates the gray areas guided by her feminist thought.

A feminist critique of hip-hop has to be able to deal with the gray areas. As Joan Morgan said, "I needed a feminism brave enough to f— with the grays. . . . I am down . . . for a feminism that demands we assume responsibility for our lives. . . . A functional feminism for myself and my sistas—[is] one that seeks empowerment on spiritual, material, physical, and emotional levels."[14] Hill talks about her love for the culture and for men while holding in balance her love for herself and women. Morgan says she needs a feminism "that would allow us to continue loving ourselves and the brothers who hurt us without letting race loyalty buy us early tombstones."[15] This is where Hill is: she loves herself and the misguided men who are a part of the hip-hop industry, but they must be confronted and hip-hop must be exorcised. She loves hip-hop enough to critique it. A healthy feminist critique of hip-hop culture and the hip-hop industry for Hill and Morgan is rooted in love. As Paul says in Galatians 4:16, "Have I now become your enemy by telling you the truth?" To tell the truth does appear to make feminists an enemy of hip-hop.

What we hear and see throughout Hill's journey on *The Miseducation of Lauryn Hill* and continued on *MTV Unplugged 2.0* is her work of defining herself in opposition to the culture's imposition of who it thinks she should be. She is fighting back, using what Collins calls "fighting words," words of resistance. As we engage hip-hop culture, a central part of that engagement must be a critique that fights against the objectification of women's bodies and the glorification of capitalism, violence, misogyny, and patriarchy. "The struggle of Black feminist thought for self-definition and self-determination constitutes a Black feminist praxis, a search for ideas that inform practice and practice that simultaneously shapes ideas."[16] This is a circular relationship in that thought and action feed off each other. As Hill develops ideas, she also demonstrates how those ideas have informed her life. When you listen to a song like "Zion," you see how her ideas and worldview are constructed in such a way as to inform her liberating praxis.

Hill and other hip-hop feminists, like myself, are in essence engaging in a conversation that we consider critical social theory. "What makes critical social theory 'critical' is its commitment to justice, for one's own group and/or for other groups."[17] As Hill and others speak with women and then share their critical reflection, they help us recast our gaze in relation to hip-hop. The resulting conversation calls out the potential and literal destructive tendencies of the culture. Patricia Hill Collins calls what Hill does breaking silence: "Breaking silence enables individual African-American women to reclaim humanity in a system that gains part of its strength by objectifying Black women."[18]

How is a woman's humanity respected and supported in hip-hop culture? How is a woman's humanity attacked and potentially destroyed by hip-hop culture? On the one hand, the role hip-hop culture plays in the development of a healthy respect for a woman's humanity needs to be affirmed. On the other hand, where it is destructive, it must be challenged. Both fans and members of the hip-hop nation cannot stand idly by in defense of what is destructive. This isn't an all-or-nothing proposition; it is filled with tension, but it is a tension that has to be worked out. One can't either defend or condemn hip-hop culture. Rather, both must be done. Moving to either extreme has the potential for silencing voices and stymieing the conversation.

As Hill engages in hip-hop while loving and talking back to hip-hop culture, she is invoking her authority as an artist and a victim. She, like so many African American women, has felt the dehumanizing effects of hip-hop. As she breaks the silence, she is making an epistemological statement about what she knows via her own experience. She is hip-hop. She has "succeeded" in the hip-hop industry while trying to protect hip-hop culture. To put it the way my momma would, "She knows what she is talking about." Her critique is from an outsider within. Collins describes the outsider-within position as

> social locations or border spaces occupied by groups of unequal power. Individuals gain or lose identities as "outsiders-within" by their placement in these social locations. . . . Outsiders-within spaces are riddled with contradictions. . . . The outsider-within location describes a particular knowledge/power relationship, one of gaining knowledge about or of a dominant group without gaining full power accorded to members of that group.[19]

Hill's critique has an outsider-within voice. She has gained access, but she is not Wyclef (the leader of the Fugees). She doesn't have a crew; she is not an industry insider. She is sitting on the inside as an outsider, critiquing the culture from the margins while being considered successful. She is struggling with what the hip-hop industry has done to her and what this means for her and hip-hop culture. She is struggling with what it means to be successful in the hip-hop industry while being true to hip-hop culture. As Collins suggests, the outsider-within position is filled with contradictions. These contradictions don't work against the person occupying this position but rather empower him or her to see that things aren't black and white. There is a gray zone that all of us who are in relationship with hip-hop have to address.

Track 7: To Zion or Hell?

To critique what we love is difficult, but it's an act of empowerment and authenticity. To love and respect something motivates a healthy critique that tends not to be malicious and careless. In the case of Hill, she is an empowered critic. As both a member of hip-hop and a product of hip-hop, she is calling hip-hop culture and the hip-hop industry to task.

Quite frankly, her critique of hip-hop asks, is hip-hop life-giving or is it taking life? Is it adding value to the community or taking life out of the community? Hill shares how she struggled concerning her son. Hip-hop asked Hill to sacrifice her child for a career, and she said no. She became pregnant at what appeared to be an inopportune time. Her handlers thought that having the child would adversely affect her career. Hill was asked to make a choice. She says she was told to put her career over the life of her unborn child. But she chose to use her heart. She chose to have the child. She chose life.

In the song "Zion," she talks about the birth of her child, Zion. She refers to how God chose her and her son. In this discourse and struggle, you hear Mary, as she too had to struggle about a child she would bring into the world to save the world. Zion for Hill is a type of savior in that he helped her see what life was really all about; life isn't about money, fame, or making it in the hip-hop game. Life for Hill is about family, love, truth, transparency, and relationships. Hill's ideas move us to see children as special and divine. This is oppositional knowledge and critique at the same time. She redefines the role of a mother in hip-hop as not "somebody's baby's momma" but a vessel of God who has been divinely chosen to give life. In the end, she says thank you to God for choosing her to give life to the grace of God in a child.

As much as hip-hop is redeeming and a financial blessing to the community, it also glorifies violence, misogyny, and materialism. The lifting up of these three as glamorous values to be embraced tells the African American community and others to sacrifice Zion. In this case, Zion not only represents the child of Hill but also points to the children of the inner city who pattern their lifestyles after those in the hip-hop industry. Young children, teenagers, and young adults who engage the hip-hop industry must be taught to choose life over death, just as Hill chose life over death. Jesus came to offer life, whereas the devil came to kill, steal, and destroy (John 10:10). When the hip-hop industry takes hip-hop to an extreme at the expense of life, it has to be critiqued and held accountable. It is appropriate to call hip-hop out in this context. The hip-hop industry pushed Hill to abort her baby. How many young men and women are being "aborted" by drive-by shootings, gang violence, poverty, prison, sexism, misogyny, and the other ills that the hip-hop industry glorifies?

To effectively critique hip-hop, we have to move beyond how many times the B-word or the F-word is used or the sexual images on a video. We have to deconstruct the miseducation that is going on via hip-hop.

Hill helps us break the silence. We can't be silent. If Zion is to have a full and fruitful life, then the role of hip-hop as a positive and negative influence must be engaged. Collins says, "Understanding the significance of breaking the silence by invoking the authority of experience requires examining how knowledge is constructed within unjust power relations. Domination, whether of race, class, gender, sexuality, or nationality, produces public and private knowledges on both sides of power relations."[20] In essence, we are talking about constructing new bodies of knowledge. To effectively critique hip-hop, we have to move beyond how many times the B-word or the F-word is used or the sexual images on a video. We have to deconstruct the miseducation that is going on via hip-hop. The mixed messages in hip-hop that mess up young people must be explained. Ways of knowing and being must be changed. Values and norms must be corrected. This calls for a Zion-like critique; we have to use our head and our heart in the critique. Moving beyond a limited critique to a full-scale revaluing of hip-hop culture requires "fighting words" used in love. God loved the world by offering the world a new way to salvation: faith and grace. What will we offer hip-hop?

Getting in Touch with Hip-Hop

Albums

Ambassador, The. *The Thesis*. Cross Movement, 2005.

Cee Lo Green. *Cee Lo Green . . . Is the Soul Machine*. Arista, 2004.

Hill, Lauryn. *The Miseducation of Lauryn Hill*. Ruffhouse/Columbia, 1998.

————. *MTV Unplugged 2.0*. Columbia, 2002.

Jay-Z. *Kingdom Come*. Roc-A-Fella, 2006.

Films

Brown Sugar. Directed by Rick Famuyiwa. Fox Searchlight, 2002.

MTV Unplugged 2.0: Lauryn Hill. Directed by Joe De Maio. New York: Columbia Music Video, 2002.

Hip-Hop: Beyond Beats and Rhymes. Directed by Byron Hurt. Media Education Foundation, 2006.

Jay-Z: Fade to Black. Directed by Patrick Paulson and Michael John Warren. Roc-A-Fella, 2004.

conclusion

From Gil Scott-Heron to Mos Def

In this final word, I return to my own journey and how powerful hip-hop culture has been in my life. I invite you to walk with me through the work of Gil Scott-Heron and Mos Def. This chapter is a bit autobiographical; I invite you to peek in on my spiritual journey as a preacher, theologian, sociologist, and defender of hip-hop culture.

I Still Love Her

We return again to the question that opens *Brown Sugar*, one of my favorite movies: so when did you fall in love with hip-hop? Every time I watch this movie—which is often—it takes me back to my affair with hip-hop. I call it an affair because that is what it feels like sometimes: I have to apologize for her, hide her, and act like we don't even know each other. When I am in some circles, hip-hop is my mistress. I am judged because I listen to, endorse, and at times dress like, talk like, walk like, live like, and write like hip-hop. My love for hip-hop makes me defend her. I know I love hip-hop most when I am angered when hip-hop is attacked or sucker punched by someone who is judging hip-hop without ever getting to know hip-hop.

Track 1: Message to the Messengers: A Preacher and Hip-Hop

At the close of this book, I go back to the beginning of hip-hop. I start with Gil Scott-Heron. He was clear that there has to be a word from the elders to the present generation of what we now call hip-hop. Hip-hop is the child of the blues. The child that has grown up must look back to the parent, and a dialogue must be established. This dialogue isn't the parent lecturing the adult child; rather,

131

it is an appreciation of each other as the parent looks across the table at the child who is all grown up. There must be some pride on the part of the parent for what the child has become. But along with the pride is a tension. The child has become its own being, and the parent is tempted to critique the child. This critique is necessary; this tension is a part of the relationship. This tension can't be avoided. Both pride and critique are needed if they are going to understand each other and appreciate each other for the ways they are similar and different.

As an African American male in my mid-forties, I look at hip-hop from a much different perspective than its peers. I am a child of the 1960s who was raised on rhythm and blues and funk. I raised my hands at the Parliament and Bootsy Collins concert, and now I am the elder in the room at hip-hop concerts. I love what hip-hop has become, while I am critical of its failures. My joy and disappointment are tempered by the fact that I remember hip-hop is art. It is not meant to do all that I and others may want it to do. It is a culture or sub-culture, and my critique includes my generational peers. We must take some of the blame, if not most of the blame, for the ways our adult child has come up short. We raised the artists and the cultural icons. We missed the opportunity to teach them about their history and welcome them into the church. We missed the opportunity to pastor them.

As my generational peers critique hip-hop and the hip-hop generation, the generational divide widens. In the final analysis, we need each other and can benefit from a restored relationship. Michael Dyson sums it up this way: "The generational conflict between black males has turned ugly. Older black men routinely put young black males down for their clothes, their music, and their corrupt values. Younger black men protest that their elders are stuck in the past and lack appreciation for their contributions and struggles. The truth is that older and younger black men have a lot to gain from each other."[1] What has gotten ugly can be made prettier if we are willing to reach out and hear the cry of hip-hop. If we don't hear the lament, we can't wipe away the tears and deal with the pain the hip-hop generation is feeling. How would you like it if you felt your elders had abandoned you?

Track 2: Finding Forever: A Theologian and Hip-Hop

When I listen to hip-hop, I hear a theological cry. The prophets are speaking, and the cry is one of deep pain and emptiness, for the culture and capitalism have sold hip-hop a bill of goods. Artists will not find wholeness, peace, joy, or God in material things. There is an empty disappointment in hip-hop as they fight for a prize that is no prize at all. It is an empty feeling to be the star of the show and find yourself lonely—for to be at the top is really the bottom. What do you do when what you have fought for, what you thought would fulfill you, leaves you unfulfilled?

Maybe I am overstating my case, but then again maybe I am not. I have found in my lifetime that joy, peace, and fulfillment aren't found in things but rather in relationships. The ultimate relationship is with Jesus Christ. This isn't about consciousness or God-knowledge; it is about a saving relationship with Jesus Christ. As much as there is good in hip-hop culture, how does one move from the good to God? A relationship with the one and only true God could be more explicit in the music and the message. There is holy hip-hop, but I am not sure holy hip-hop artists aren't captivated by some of the same things that drive secular hip-hop. (That is another book.) We have to work to develop Christian theologians who are of the hip-hop nation. When I listen to the Ambassador and the Cross Movement crew, I am impressed and see us moving in the right direction.

When I listen to hip-hop, I hear a theological cry. The prophets are speaking, and the cry is one of deep pain and emptiness, for the culture and capitalism have sold hip-hop a bill of goods.

The problem with holy hip-hop is that these artists are caught in a pickle: they are compelled to be on the theological right and so they appear to be ultraconservative. This compulsion is an apparent reaction to the church's critique of hip-hop. The church has rejected hip-hop culture, and the voice of G. Craig Lewis has been at the forefront of this assault. As a result, holy hip-hop has had to appear to be pure and biblically sound at all costs. The very appearance of being too much like secular hip-hop is a death knell to the ministry of holy hip-hop. So while holy hip-hop looks and sounds like the broader hip-hop culture, the lyrics are markedly different (as they should be), but it is also theologically conservative. This is especially true of artists like Da Truth, Lecrae, FLAME, and the Ambassador. When I listen to this art, I wonder, what if they were free, from a theological standpoint, to explore more diverse issues without having stones thrown at them? There are those like Pigeon John who appear to be freer with the art, but he is the exception that proves the rule. The two—secular hip-hop and holy hip-hop—must meet in an effort to define a healthy Christian theological perspective. This perspective needs to come through the culture with wholeness and with a biblical soundness that is liberating and that lifts up the saving message of Jesus Christ as Lord and Savior.

Track 3: The Doctor's Advocate: A Sociologist and Hip-Hop

I have been a supporter of hip-hop—both secular and holy—as I have matured into my forties. This is an awkward position. For instance, sitting in my car this morning listening to *Tha Carter III*, I received looks from those who pulled up beside me. I have come to find it comical and painful at the same time. I want to say I don't care what people think about me, but in reality I do care. I care because on one level I think about how disconnected we all are from one another. I have to speak to a graduation class at church this Saturday, and I am working on a piece called "What Do Jesus and Lil Wayne Have in Common?" I couldn't do this piece if I didn't listen to Lil Wayne. When I announce this title, I am sure parents and high school seniors are going to sit up in their seats. As a socio-theologian who believes that theology is birthed in the culture, I argue that we can't be conversant with the theological musing in the culture if we aren't conversant with the culture.

This Saturday's experiment and my engagement with hip-hop culture are essential if I hope to seek and save that which is lost. I advocate a conversation with hip-hop culture because in essence we are in conversation with those socio-theological forces that touch those both inside and outside the church. Something happens on *Tha Carter III* that doesn't normally happen in church. Lil Wayne manages to talk about everything from oral sex to the crisis of Katrina in thirteen tracks. To speak to the vast spectrum of one's life in an hour is powerful. The church is bent on limiting the story or conversation, but not hip-hop.

So as a PhD and socio-theologian, I think there is much we can learn from hip-hop about how to effectively communicate—not just with the hip-hop culture but with the larger culture as well. Hip-hop knows how to use concepts, metaphors, and the power of storytelling to affect life. Hip-hop artists know how to speak into the lives of their followers as they riff with the ebbs and flows of popular culture. This ability to be integrative is amazing and amazingly absent in the church. The church has bought into a Western model of segregating the sacred and the secular. We have established a compartmentalized theology that speaks within the four walls of a church but not to the streets outside the church. If the church were as successful as hip-hop at communicating with youth and young adults, we wouldn't have the problem we have with hip-hop. I don't buy the argument that the gospel can't be as attractive as hip-hop. If Jesus attracted thousands with no iTunes, no publicist, and no sound system, what can we do? We can learn from hip-hop and find out how it is touching what we are missing.

Track 4: Murder Was the Case That They Gave Me: A Defender of Hip-Hop

I'm often asked how I can defend hip-hop when it glorifies death. And in a way the question amazes me. Those asking the question don't seem to recognize all the ways our popular culture glorifies death and violence. Violent movies and video games are extremely popular, and our military industry dwarfs the entire economies of many countries around the world! The larger question is this: how can hip-hop even begin to talk about love when its followers are hated, despised, and left in poverty-stricken communities? How can hip-hop have any ray of hope? The fact is that America has turned its back on the poor. (This is yet another book.) Just read the works of authors like William J. Wilson, bell hooks, Alex Koklowitz, and Robert Michael Franklin. Then finish off with Kenneth J. Neubeck's *When Welfare Disappears: The Case for Economic Human Rights.* These authors provide a convincing argument that hip-hop should not be charged with murder. Rather, America should be charged with neglecting the poor and leaving them to die in the inner city. So I still defend hip-hop. Hip-hop is a child of America. The child has some guilt by association, but the parent has the greater responsibility.

Hip-hop has been victimized by the sin of being an art form raised in a violent country that has quarantined poverty and the poor.

Hip-hop is more victim than perpetrator. Hip-hop is caught in a twisted mess as it feeds into America's greed and thirst to conquer. Hip-hop has been victimized by the sin of being an art form raised in a violent country that has quarantined poverty and the poor. If you read Octavia Butler's *Parable of the Sower*, maybe what I am saying will come to light. Or simply watch the movie *New Jack City*, and you will see the conditions in which hip-hop was birthed and has matured. Hip-hop isn't killing anybody. The deaths we see in the inner city are larger than hip-hop. Systemic oppression and poverty are killing our young people. The absence of a prophetic church is killing our young people. Read Cornel West's classic book *Prophesy Deliverance! An Afro-American Revolutionary Christianity* along with Marvin A. McMickle's *Where Have All the Prophets Gone? Reclaiming Prophetic Preaching in America*, and ask yourself, does the church today look like the church of Jesus Christ? How is the church operating in a liberating, prophetic way to combat the ills of an America that worships at the temple of Mammon in the form of capitalism gone wild?

Track 5: Get Free or Die Trying versus Get Rich or Die Trying: Where Do We Go from Here—Chaos or Community?

The issue is the absence of prophets in the pulpit. In her book *Name It and Claim It? Prosperity Preaching in the Black Church*, Stephanie Y. Mitchem talks about "spiritual longing."[2] She suggests that African Americans are longing for justice and a part of the American pie. The prosperity preachers have gotten rich off a bling-bling gospel that sounds more like 50 Cent than Martin Luther King Jr. The profit-ic church is no more or less bling than hip-hop.[3] The prosperity-gospel preachers have sold out the church for personal gain and community decay. Major churches have abandoned the inner city, not just by relocating to the suburbs but also by not fighting for justice. While hip-hop is a child of capitalism and shouldn't be held to the same standard as the church, to some extent it is doing more for the community than many of our churches.

At least the hip-hop industry is providing jobs for millions of young people. Hip-hop provides hope for a future that can be realized with talent and hard work. Master P and so many others succeeded by selling CDs out of the trunk of their car. While hip-hop doesn't offer the God of salvation, it can provide food for some people's tables. Maybe if the church took the social gospel—which is really the gospel—seriously, maybe our young people wouldn't have to turn to hip-hop. Instead, they could turn to a church and a God who saves, feeds, and provides. The church has to embrace the agenda of being an agent of freedom. When the gospel message is reduced to self-help theology, we have moved from being free to getting rich, and this wealth does not bring freedom.

> *Hip-hop has been seduced, like the church, into a materialistic, individualistic, capitalistic, patriarchal model. The two must come together and seek liberation, freedom, and salvation from a God who saves. Jesus saves, not hip-hop, and not the church.*

Martin Luther King Jr. asked the question in his final full-length book: where do we go from here? As the civil rights movement moved to economic rights, he asked, will we move toward chaos or community? Forty years after his death, we have the answer. As the church abandoned the next leg of the struggle, we exchanged prophets for profits in the pulpit, and the struggle has been left looking for a leader.

Track 6: God's Sons and Daughters: Redeeming Hip-Hop or Will Hip-Hop Redeem Us?

If hip-hop has a role in the liberation of African Americans and other people, then the church is going to have to call hip-hop back home and sit with her. Hip-hop comes out of the struggle and pain of the African diasporic community. Hip-hop has been seduced, like the church, into a materialistic, individualistic, capitalistic, patriarchal model. The two must come together and seek liberation, freedom, and salvation from a God who saves. Jesus saves, not hip-hop, and not the church. God has chosen to use his church for the work of salvation. God has chosen to work through the church. In some instances, the church has fallen into a form of idolatry, and like hip-hop, it needs an exorcism. If this exorcism of both the church and hip-hop is to come, the church should lead the way. The church should extend its hands up to God and begin to recite that famous text from 2 Chronicles 7:14:

If my people, who are called by my name, will humble themselves and pray and seek my face and turn from their wicked ways, then will I hear from heaven and will forgive their sin and will heal their land.

It is time for the church to stop blaming hip-hop or pointing the finger; we need to take some time to pray. Maybe at the end of this book you were expecting some grand theological revelation. I hope this doesn't disappoint you, but this is it. We need to pray. The church needs to seek God's face about how to hear God in hip-hop, how to minister to the hip-hop generation, and how we can be saved and save simultaneously. This will require that the church humble itself. Maybe we don't have it all right. Maybe in our righteous arrogance we haven't heard all God is trying to say. Maybe, just maybe, we need to be humble enough to hear God tell us where we may have gone wrong. God is calling God's people, but do we hear? Is God calling us through hip-hop? Is hip-hop crying? Do we hear the pain? When we hear God and turn to God, God promises to heal our land and our people. Let the healing begin as we turn from our wicked ways and turn to God. Wickedness is not just in hip-hop; maybe there is some wickedness in the church. Let the healing begin.

notes

Introduction

1. Michael Dyson, *Holler If You Hear Me: Searching for Tupac Shakur* (New York: Basic Civitas Books, 2002), 118.

2. Spencer, as quoted in David Fillingim, *Redneck Liberation: Country Music as Theology* (Macon, GA: Mercer University Press, 2003), 3.

3. Ibid.

4. James H. Cone, *The Spirituals and the Blues: An Interpretation* (New York: Seabury Press, 1972; repr., Maryknoll, NY: Orbis, 1992).

Chapter 1: When Did You Fall in Love with Hip-Hop?

1. Bakari Kitwana, *The Hip Hop Generation: Young Blacks and the Crisis in African American Culture* (New York: Basic Civitas Books, 2003), 15.

2. Audrey Edwards and Craig. K. Polite, *Children of the Dream: The Psychology of Black Success* (New York: Doubleday, 1992).

3. Todd Boyd, *Am I Black Enough for You? Popular Culture from the 'Hood and Beyond* (Bloomington: Indiana University Press, 1997), 17.

4. Fab 5 Freddy, a.k.a. Fred Brathwaite, *Fresh Fly Flavor: Words and Phrases of the Hip-Hop Generation* (Stamford, CT: Longmeadow Press, 1992), 32: "The term hip-hop originated in the mid-1970s during the beginning stages of what is also known as rap. It was first said by DJ Hollywood, who while playing records would get on the mike and shout 'To the *hip-hop* the hippy hippy hippy hippy hop and you don't stop.'" This became common in usage as those who attended hip-hop parties referred to the parties and culture as hip-hop. The term was then popularized when the first major commercial hip-hop record, *Rapper's Delight*, started off with the phrase coined by DJ Hollywood.

5. Saul Williams, *The Dead Emcee Scrolls: The Lost Teachings of Hip-Hop* (New York: MTV, 2006), 26.

6. Jasmine Guy, *Afeni Shakur: Evolution of a Revolutionary* (New York: Atria Books, 2004), 40.

7. The Afrika Bambaataa and James Brown song "Unity" (*Unity*, Tommy Boy TB 847, 1982, 33⅓ rpm, 12-inch) sets the foundation for this chant as it defines hip-hop.

8. Theodor W. Adorno, *Essays on Music: Selected*, with introduction, commentary, and notes by Richard Leppert, new translations by Susan H. Gillespie (Berkeley: University of California Press, 2002), 114.

9. Williams, *Dead Emcee Scrolls*, 11.

10. Will Smith, *Greatest Hits*, Columbia CK 87076, 2002, compact disc.

11. Adorno, *Essays on Music*, 115.

Chapter 2: I Said a Hip-Hop

1. Fab 5 Freddy, a.k.a. Fred Brathwaite, *Fresh Fly Flavor: Words and Phrases of the Hip-Hop Generation* (Stamford, CT: Longmeadow Press, 1992), 32.

2. Russell Potter, *Spectacular Vernaculars: Hip-Hop and the Politics of Postmodernism* (Albany: State University of New York Press, 1995), 148.

3. Jeff Chang, *Can't Stop, Won't Stop: A History of the Hip-Hop Generation* (New York: St. Martin's Press, 2005).

4. Alex Ogg and David Upshal, *The Hip-Hop Years: A History of Rap* (New York: Fromm International, 2001).

5. David Toop, *The Rap Attack: African Jive to New York Hip-Hop* (Boston: South End Press, 1984); *Rap Attack 2: African Rap to Global Hip-Hop* (London: Serpent's Tail, 1994); *Rap Attack 3: African Rap to Global Hip-Hop* (London: Serpent's Tail, 2000).

6. See the *Freestyle: The Art of Rhyme*, directed by Kevin Fitzgerald (Organic Films, 2000; New York: Palm Pictures, 2004), DVD.

7. Jim Fricke and Charlie Ahearn, *Yes Yes Y'All: The Experience Music Project Oral History of Hip-Hop's First Decade* (Cambridge, MA: Da Capo Press, 2002).

8. Ibid., i.

9. Ibid., 4.

10. Ibid.

11. See *Scratch*, directed by Doug Pray (Firewalk Films, 2001; New York: Palm Pictures, 2002), DVD; and *Beat Kings: The History of Hip-Hop,* directed by Mathematics (New York: Nature Sounds, 2006), DVD.

12. Fricke and Ahearn, *Yes Yes Y'all,* 25.

13. Michael Muhammad Knight, *The Five Percenters: Islam, Hip-Hop, and the Gods of New York* (Oxford: Oneworld, 2007).

14. Kraftwerk, *Trans-Europa Express,* Capitol SW-11603, 1977, 33⅓ rpm, LP.

15. Raquel Z. Rivera, *New York Ricans from the Hip-Hop Zone* (New York: Palgrave Macmillan, 2003). Rivera does a great job telling the story of the contributions of New York Ricans to the founding of hip-hop and how hip-hop brought the working-class ethnic communities together.

16. Fricke and Ahearn, *Yes Yes Y'All,* 59.

17. Ibid., 63.

18. Ibid., 74.

19. Ibid., 76.

20. Murray Forman, *The 'Hood Comes First: Race, Space, and Place in Rap and Hip-Hop* (Middletown, CT: Wesleyan University Press, 2002), xviii.

21. Ibid., 111.

22. Alan Light, ed., *The Vibe History of Hip-Hop* (New York: Three Rivers Press, 1999), 24–25.

23. The story of Def Jam Recordings is told in Stacy Gueraseva, *Def Jam, Inc.: Russell Simmons, Rick Rubin, and the Extraordinary Story of the World's Most Influential Hip-Hop Label* (New York: One World/ Ballantine, 2005). I encourage you to read both Gueraseva's book and Russell Simmons's *Life and Def: Sex, Drugs, Money + God* (New York: Three Rivers Press, 2001).

24. Michael Dyson, *HollerIf You Hear Me: Searching for Tupac Shakur* (New York: Basic Civitas Books, 2002), 119.

25. Joan Morgan, *When Chickenheads Come Home to Roost: My Life as a Hip-Hop Feminist* (New York: Simon & Schuster, 1999), 26.

26. For the full story of Run-D.M.C. and Jam Master Jay, see Ronin Ro, *Raising Hell: The Reign, Ruin, and Redemption of Run-D.M.C. and Jam Master Jay* (New York: Amistad, 2005). For the Adidas story, see under the heading "Track 6: I See You."

27. Eithne Quinn, *Nuthin' but a "G" Thang: The Culture and Commerce of Gangsta Rap* (New York: Columbia University Press, 2004).

28. VIBE Books, *Hip-Hop Divas* (New York: Three Rivers Press, 2001).

29. Nas, "Hip-Hop Is Dead," on *Hip-Hop Is Dead*, Def Jam B0007229-02, 2006, compact disc; and T.I., "Help Is on the Way," on *T.I. vs. T.I.P.*, Atlantic 202171-2, 2007, compact disc, where T.I. says he will save hip-hop.

30. Jerry Heller, with Gil Reavill, *Ruthless: A Memoir* (New York: Simon Spotlight Entertainment, 2006), 35.

31. The story of the West is chronicled not only in Quinn's book but also in William Shaw's *Westside: The Coast-to-Coast Explosion of Hip-Hop* (New York: First Cooper Square Press, 2002). You can also read a complementary commentary to the work of Eithne Quinn in Ronin Ro's *Gangsta: Merchandising the Rhymes of Violence* (New York: St. Martin's Press, 1996). Finally, there is Joel McIver's *Ice Cube Attitude* (London: Sanctuary Publishing Limited, 2002).

32. David Banner, foreword to *Country Fried Soul: Adventures in Dirty South Hip-Hop*, by Tamara Palmer (San Francisco: Backbeat Books, 2005), 7.

33. Palmer, *Country Fried Soul*, 61.

34. Ibid., 62.

35. Ibid.

36. A full story of the Third Coast is recorded in Roni Sarig's *Third Coast: Outkast, Timbaland, and How Hip-Hop Became a Southern Thing* (Cambridge, MA: Da Capo Press, 2007).

37. Tony Mitchell, ed., *Global Noise: Rap and Hip-Hop outside the USA* (Middletown, CT: Wesleyan University Press, 2001), 1.

38. Ian Condry, *Hip-Hop Japan: Rap and the Paths of Cultural Globalization* (Durham, NC: Duke University Press, 2006), 1.

Chapter 3: R U Still Down?

1. Joan Morgan, *When Chickenheads Come Home to Roost: My Life as a Hip-Hop Feminist* (New York: Simon & Schuster, 1999), 72, 80.

2. Will Coleman, "Tribal Talk: African Ancestral Spirituality as a Resource for Wholeness," in *Teaching African American Religions*, ed. Carolyn M. Jones and Theodore Louis Trost (New York: Oxford University Press, 2005), 168.

3. Stic.man, *The Art of Emceeing* (Atlanta: Boss Up, 2005), 13.

4. Will Coleman, *Tribal Talk: Black Theology, Hermeneutics, and African/American Ways of Telling the Story* (University Park: Pennsylvania State University Press, 2000), 160–61.

5. Morgan, *When Chickenheads Come Home to Roost*, 26.

6. James H. Cone, *The Spirituals and the Blues: An Interpretation* (New York: Seabury Press, 1972; repr., Maryknoll, NY: Orbis, 1992), 106.

7. Coleman, *Tribal Talk*, 193.

8. William J. Wilson, *The Declining Significance of Race* (Chicago: University of Chicago Press, 1980).

9. www.mack10.com/bio.aspx (accessed 2005).

10. Robin d.g. Kelley, *Yo' Mama's Disfunktional! Fighting the Culture Wars in Urban America* (Boston: Beacon, 1998), 4.

11. Ibid., 81.

12. William J. Wilson, *The Ghetto Underclass: Social Science Perspectives* (Newbury Park, CA: Sage, 1993), 12.

13. bell hooks, *Where We Stand* (New York: Routledge, 2000), 2.

14. Todd Boyd, *The New H.N.I.C. (Head Niggas in Charge): The Death of Civil Rights and the Reign of Hip-Hop* (New York: New York University Press, 2004), 3.

15. Cornel West, *Prophesy Deliverance! An Afro-American Revolutionary Christianity* (Philadelphia: Westminster Press, 1982), 143.

16. C. Eric Lincoln and Lawrence H. Mamiya, *The Black Church in the African American Experience* (Durham, NC: Duke University Press, 1990), 384.

17. Michael Eric Dyson, *Holler if You Hear Me: Searching for Tupac Shakur* (New York: Basic Civitas Books, 2002), 4.

18. Afeni Shakur, *Evolution of a Revolutionary* (New York: Atria Books, 2004), 40.

19. Arrested Development, "Fishin' for Religion," on *3 Years, 5 Months, and 2 Days in the Life of*, Chrysalis, CDP-21929, 1992, compact disc.

20. The attraction to hip-hop of whites is charted in Bakari Kitwana, *Why White Kids Love Hip-Hop: Wangstas, Wiggers, Wannabes, and the New Reality of Race in America* (New York: Basic Civitas Books, 2005).

21. Bakari Kitwana, *The Hip-Hop Generation: Young Blacks and the Crisis in African American Culture* (New York: Basic Civitas Books, 2003), 155.

22. Boyd, *New H.N.I.C.*, 152.

23. Wyatt Tee Walker, *Somebody's Calling My Name* (Valley Forge, PA: Judson, 1983), 15.

24. Cone, *Spirituals and the Blues*, 6.

25. Ian Condry, *Hip-Hop Japan: Rap and the Paths of Cultural Globalization* (Durham, NC: Duke University Press, 2006), 24–25; and Tony Mitchell, ed., *Global Noise: Rap and Hip-Hop outside the USA* (Middletown, CT: Wesleyan University Press, 2001), 1–2.

26. Imani Perry, *Prophets of the Hood: Politics and Poetics in Hip-Hop* (Durham, NC: Duke University Press, 2004), 10.

27. Molefi Kete Asante, *The Afrocentric Idea* (Philadelphia: Temple University Press, 1987), 11.

28. Ngugi wa Thiong'o, *Decolonising the Mind* (Portsmouth, NH: Heinemann, 1986), 13–14.

29. Ibid., 14–15.

30. Dyson, *Holler if You Hear Me*, 119.

31. Albert Murray, *The Hero and the Blues* (New York: Vintage, 1995), 21.

32. Ibid., 22.

33. Ibid.

34. Patricia Hill Collins, *Fighting Words: Black Women and the Search for Justice* (Minneapolis: University of Minnesota Press, 1998).

35. Murray, *Hero and the Blues*, 36.

36. Ibid., 39.

37. Young Buck, *Buck the World*, G-Unit/Interscope B0008030-01, 2007, compact disc.

38. Murray, *Hero and the Blues*, 59.

39. Eddie S. Glaude Jr., *Exodus! Religion, Race, and Nation in Early Nineteenth-Century Black America* (Chicago: University of Chicago Press, 2000).

40. Murray, *Hero and the Blues*, 61.

41. Ibid.

42. Quoted in Jon Michael Spencer, *Blues and Evil* (Knoxville: University of Tennessee Press, 1993), 39.

43. Ibid.

44. Ibid., quoting from Leonard Goines, "The Blues as Black Therapy," *Black World*, November 1973, 31.

45. Cone, *Spirituals and the Blues*, 97.

46. Ibid., 98.

47. Ibid., 100.

48. Morgan, *When Chickenheads Come Home to Roost*, 26.

49. Cone, *Spirituals and the Blues*, 103.

50. Ibid., 105.

51. Ibid., 106.

52. Ibid., 107.

53. Ibid., 110.

54. Ibid., 111.

55. Ibid., 115.

56. Ibid., 116.

57. Morgan, *When Chickenheads Come Home to Roost*, 73–75.

58. Cone, *Spirituals and the Blues*, 117.

59. Morgan, *When Chickenheads Come Home to Roost*, 72.

60. Cone, *Spirituals and the Blues*, 125.

61. Robin Sylvan, *Traces of the Spirit: The Religious Dimensions of Popular Music* (New York: New York University Press, 2002), 3.

62. Spencer, *Blues and Evil*, 35.

63. Ibid., 15.

Chapter 4: I Used to Love Her and I Still Love Her

1. Common, *Be*, GOOD/Geffen B0004670-02, 2005, compact disc; and *Finding Forever*, GOOD/Geffen B0009671-02, 2007, compact disc.

2. Common Sense, "I Used to Love Her," on *Resurrection*, Relativity 88561-1208-2, 1994, compact disc.

3. Jon Michael Spencer, *Blues and Evil* (Knoxville: University of Tennessee Press, 1993), xxv.

4. Houston A. Baker Jr., *Black Studies, Rap, and the Academy* (Chicago: University of Chicago Press, 1993), 84.

5. Mos Def, "Fear Not of Man," on *Black on Both Sides*, Rawkus P2-50141, 1999, compact disc.

6. William Jelani Cobb, *To the Break of Dawn: A Freestyle on the Hip-Hop Aesthetic* (New York: New York University Press, 2007), 9–10.

7. Kool Moe Dee, *There's a God on the Mic: The True 50 Greatest MCs* (New York: Thunder's Mouth Press, 2003).

8. Cobb, *To the Break of Dawn*, 87.

9. Ibid.

10. Joan Morgan, *When Chickenheads Come Home to Roost: My Life as a Hip-Hop Feminist.* (New York: Simon & Schuster, 1999), 72.

11. Ibid., 73.

12. Ibid.

13. Ibid., 74.

14. Michael Dyson, *Know What I Mean? Reflections on Hip-Hop* (New York: Basic Civitas Books, 2007), xxi.

15. Ibid., 135.

16. Patricia Hill Collins, *Black Sexual Politics: African Americans, Gender, and the New Racism* (New York: Routledge, 2005), 126.

17. Dyson, *Know What I Mean?*, 21.

18. Ibid., 22.

19. Collins, *Black Sexual Politics*, 182.

20. Lil Jon and the East Side Boys, "Get Low," on *The Kings of Crunk*, TVT TV-2370-2, 2002, compact disc.

Chapter 5: "Slippin' and Slidin' I'm about to Give Up"

1. Wilfred Cantwell Smith, *What Is Scripture? A Comparative Approach* (Minneapolis: Fortress, 1993), 18.

2. William A. Graham, *Beyond the Written Word: Oral Aspects of Scripture in the History of Religion* (New York: Cambridge University Press, 1987), 5.

3. Ibid., 65.

4. Ibid., 67.

5. Ibid., 75.

6. Ibid., 114–15.

7. Ibid., 160.

8. Ibid., 155.

9. Ibid., 167.

10. James H. Cone, *The Spirituals and the Blues: An Interpretation* (New York: Seabury Press, 1972; repr., Maryknoll, NY: Orbis, 1992), 100.

11. Jon Michael Spencer, "Overview of American Pop Music in Theological Perspective," in *Theomusicology* (special issue of *Black Sacred Music: A Journal of Theomusicology* [Spring 1994]) (Durham, NC: Duke University Press, 1994), 205.

12. Ibid., 216.

13. Larry Joseph Kreitzer, *The New Testament in Fiction and Film: On Reversing the Hermeneutical Flow* (Sheffield, UK: Sheffield Academic Press, 1993), 19.

14. Anthony B. Pinn, *Why, Lord? Suffering and Evil in Black Theology* (New York: Continuum, 1995), 116.

15. Ibid., 121.

16. Ibid., 134.

17. DMX, as told to Smokey D. Fontaine, *E.A.R.L.: Ever Always Real Life: The Autobiography of DMX* (New York: Harper, 2003), 41.

18. Ibid., 69.

19. Ibid., 277.

20. Ibid., 291.

21. Ibid.

22. "Prayer," on *It's Dark and Hell Is Hot* (Def Jam 542 437-2, 1998, compact disc), as quoted in ibid., 334.

23. Ibid.

24. Smith, *What Is Scripture?*, 18.

Chapter 6: God Skipped Past the Church

1. Gordon Lynch, *Understanding Theology and Popular Culture* (Malden, MA: Blackwell, 2004), 184.

2. Talib Kweli, *Eardrum*, Blacksmith/Warner Bros. 277244-2, 2007, compact disc. All Kweli quotes in this chapter come from this album.

3. Will Coleman, *Tribal Talk: Black Theology, Hermeneutics, and African/American Ways of Telling the Story* (University Park: Pennsylvania State University Press, 2000), 194.

4. Michael Muhammad Knight, *The Five Percenters: Islam, Hip-Hop, and the Gods of New York* (Oxford: Oneworld, 2007).

5. Mark L. Chapman, *Christianity on Trial: African-American Religious Thought before and after Black Power* (Maryknoll, NY: Orbis, 1996), 8.

Chapter 7: *The Miseducation of Lauryn Hill*

1. Erykah Badu featuring Common, "Love of My Life (An Ode to Hip-Hop)," on *Brown Sugar*, music from the motion picture soundtrack, MCA 088 113 02802, 2002, compact disc.

2. Gil Scott-Heron, "Message to the Messengers," on *Spirits*, TVT TVT 4310-2, 1994, compact disc.

3. Gwendolyn Pough, ed., *Home Girls Make Some Noise: Hip-Hop Feminism Anthology* (Mira Loma, CA: Parker, 2007), viii.

4. Ibid., vii.

5. Patricia Hill Collins, *Fighting Words: Black Women and the Search for Justice* (Minneapolis: University of Minnesota Press, 1998), 193.

6. Lauryn Hill, *MTV Unplugged 2.0*, Columbia CK 69035, 2002, compact disc.

7. Cee Lo Green, "I'm Selling Soul," on *Cee Lo Green . . . Is the Soul Machine*, Arista 82876 52111 2, 2004, compact disc.

8. Will Coleman, *Tribal Talk: Black Theology, Hermeneutics, and African/American Ways of Telling the Story* (University Park: Pennsylvania State University Press, 2000), 171.

9. Bakari Kitwana, *Why White Kids Love Hip-Hop: Wangstas, Wiggers, Wannabes, and the New Reality of Race in America* (New York: Basic Civitas Books, 2005).

10. Billie Holiday, "Strange Fruit," on *The Best of Billie Holiday: The Millennium Collection*, Hip-O 314 589 995-2, 2002, compact disc.

11. Carter G. Woodson, *The Miseducation of the Negro* (Trenton, NJ: Africa World Press, 1993), xiii.

12. Collins, *Fighting Words*, 88.

13. Ibid., 89.

14. Joan Morgan, *When Chickenheads Come Home to Roost: My Life as a Hip-Hop Feminist* (New York: Simon & Schuster, 1999), 59, 61.

15. Ibid., 36.

16. Collins, *Fighting Words*, 89.

17. Ibid., xiv.

18. Ibid., 47.

19. Ibid., 5–6.

20. Ibid., 49.

Conclusion

1. Michael E. Dyson, *Know What I Mean? Reflections on Hip-Hop* (New York: Basic Civitas Books, 2007), 139.

2. Stephanie Y. Mitchem, *Name It and Claim It? Prosperity Preaching in the Black Church* (Cleveland: Pilgrim Press, 2007), 33.

3. We aren't going to deal with the sexism in the church. Please read Kelly Brown Douglas, Jacquelyn Grant, and Emile Townes. See especially Cheryl Townsend Gilkes, *If It Wasn't for the Women* (Maryknoll, NY: Orbis, 2000); and Daphne C. Wiggins, *Righteous Content: Black Women's Perspectives of Church and Faith* (New York: New York University Press, 2006). These two books lay out the case of sexism in the church; read them and weep, then dry your tears and change it.

bibliography

Books

Adorno, Theodor W. *Essays on Music: Selected*. With introduction, commentary, and notes by Richard Leppert, new translations by Susan H. Gillespie. Berkeley: University of California Press, 2002.

Asante, Molefi Kete. *The Afrocentric Idea*. Philadelphia: Temple University Press, 1987.

Baker, Houston A., Jr. *Black Studies, Rap, and the Academy*. Chicago: University of Chicago Press, 1993.

Boyd, Todd. *Am I Black Enough for You? Popular Culture from the 'Hood and Beyond*. Bloomington: Indiana University Press, 1997.

————. *The New H.N.I.C. (Head Niggas in Charge): The Death of Civil Rights and the Reign of Hip-Hop*. New York: New York University Press, 2004.

Chang, Jeff. *Can't Stop, Won't Stop: A History of the Hip-Hop Generation*. New York: St. Martin's Press, 2005.

————. *Total Chaos: The Art and Aesthetics of Hip-Hop*. New York: Basic Civitas Books, 2007.

Chapman, Mark L. *Christianity on Trial: African-American Religious Thought before and after Black Power*. Maryknoll, NY: Orbis, 1996.

Cobb, William Jelani. *To the Break of Dawn: A Freestyle on the Hip-Hop Aesthetic*. New York: New York University Press, 2007.

Coleman, Will. "Tribal Talk: African Ancestral Spirituality as a Resource for Wholeness." In *Teaching African American Religions*, edited by Carolyn M. Jones and Theodore Louis Trost, 155–74. New York: Oxford University Press, 2005.

———. *Tribal Talk: Black Theology, Hermeneutics, and African/American Ways of Telling the Story.* University Park: Pennsylvania State University Press, 2000.

Collins, Patricia Hill. *Black Sexual Politics: African Americans, Gender, and the New Racism.* New York: Routledge, 2005.

———. *Fighting Words: Black Women and the Search for Justice.* Minneapolis: University of Minnesota Press, 1998.

Condry, Ian. *Hip-Hop Japan: Rap and the Paths of Cultural Globalization.* Durham, NC: Duke University Press, 2006.

Cone, James H. *The Spirituals and the Blues: An Interpretation.* New York: Seabury Press, 1972. Reprint, Maryknoll, NY: Orbis, 1992.

DMX, as told to Smokey D. Fontaine. *E.A.R.L.: Ever Always Real Life: The Autobiography of DMX.* New York: Harper, 2003.

Dyson, Michael Eric. *Holler If You Hear Me: Searching for Tupac Shakur.* New York: Basic Civitas Books, 2002.

———. *Know What I Mean? Reflections on Hip-Hop.* New York: Basic Civitas Books, 2007.

Edwards, Audrey, and Craig K. Polite. *Children of the Dream: The Psychology of Black Success.* New York: Doubleday, 1992.

Fab 5 Freddy, a.k.a. Fred Brathwaite. *Fresh Fly Flavor: Words and Phrases of the Hip-Hop Generation.* Stamford, CT: Longmeadow Press, 1992.

Fillingim, David. *Redneck Liberation: Country Music as Theology.* Macon, GA: Mercer University Press, 2003.

Forman, Murray. *The 'Hood Comes First: Race, Space, and Place in Rap and Hip-Hop.* Middletown, CT: Wesleyan University Press, 2002.

Fricke, Jim, and Charlie Ahearn. *Yes Yes Y'All: The Experience Music Project Oral History of Hip-Hop's First Decade.* Cambridge, MA: Da Capo Press, 2002.

Glaude, Eddie S., Jr. *Exodus! Religion, Race, and Nation in Early Nineteenth-Century Black America.* Chicago: University of Chicago Press, 2000.

Graham, William A. *Beyond the Written Word: Oral Aspects of Scripture in the History of Religion.* New York: Cambridge University Press, 1987.

Gueraseva, Stacy. *Def Jam, Inc.: Russell Simmons, Rick Rubin, and the Extraordinary Story of the World's Most Influential Hip-Hop Label.* New York: One World/Ballantine, 2005.

Guy, Jasmine. *Afeni Shakur: Evolution of a Revolutionary.* New York: Atria Books, 2004.

Heller, Jerry, with Gil Reavill. *Ruthless: A Memoir.* New York: Simon Spotlight Entertainment, 2006.

hooks, bell. *Where We Stand.* New York: Routledge, 2000.

Jones, Carolyn M., and Theodore Louis Trost. *Teaching African American Religions.* New York: Oxford University Press, 2005.

Kelley, Robin d.g. *Yo' Mama's Disfunktional! Fighting the Culture Wars in Urban America*. Boston: Beacon, 1998.

Kitwana, Bakari. *The Hip-Hop Generation: Young Blacks and the Crisis in African American Culture*. New York: Basic Civitas Books, 2003.

———. *Why White Kids Love Hip-Hop: Wangstas, Wiggers, Wannabes, and the New Reality of Race in America*. New York: Basic Civitas Books, 2005.

Knight, Michael Muhammad. *The Five Percenters: Islam, Hip-Hop, and the Gods of New York*. Oxford: Oneworld, 2007.

Kool Moe Dee. *There's a God on the Mic: The True 50 Greatest MCs*. New York: Thunder's Mouth Press, 2003.

Kreitzer, Larry Joseph. *The New Testament in Fiction and Film: On Reversing the Hermeneutical Flow*. Sheffield, UK: Sheffield Academic Press, 1993.

Light, Alan, ed. *The Vibe History of Hip-Hop*. New York: Three Rivers Press, 1999.

Lincoln, C. Eric, and Lawrence H. Mamiya. *The Black Church in the African American Experience*. Durham, NC: Duke University Press, 1990.

Lynch, Gordon. *Understanding Theology and Popular Culture*. Malden, MA: Blackwell, 2004.

McIver, Joel. *Ice Cube Attitude*. London: Sanctuary Publishing Limited, 2002.

Mitchell, Tony, ed. *Global Noise: Rap and Hip-Hop outside the USA*. Middletown, CT: Wesleyan University Press, 2001.

Mitchem, Stephanie Y. *Name It and Claim It? Prosperity Preaching in the Black Church*. Cleveland: Pilgrim Press, 2007.

Morgan, Joan. *When Chickenheads Come Home to Roost: My Life as a Hip-Hop Feminist*. New York: Simon & Schuster, 1999.

Murray, Albert. *The Hero and the Blues*. New York: Vintage, 1995.

Ogg, Alex, and David Upshal. *The Hip-Hop Years: A History of Rap*. New York: Fromm International, 2001.

Palmer, Tamara. *Country Fried Soul: Adventures in Dirty South Hip-Hop*. San Francisco: Backbeat Books, 2005.

Perry, Imani. *Prophets of the Hood: Politics and Poetics in Hip-Hop*. Durham, NC: Duke University Press, 2004.

Pinn, Anthony B. *Varieties of African-American Religious Experience*. Minneapolis: Fortress, 1998.

———. *Why, Lord? Suffering and Evil in Black Theology*. New York: Continuum, 1995.

Potter, Russell. *Spectacular Vernaculars: Hip-Hop and the Politics of Postmodernism*. Albany: State University of New York Press, 1995.

Pough, Gwendolyn, ed. *Home Girls Make Some Noise: Hip-Hop Feminism Anthology*. Mira Loma, CA: Parker, 2007.

Quinn, Eithne. *Nuthin' but a "G" Thang: The Culture and Commerce of Gangsta Rap*. New York: Columbia University Press, 2004.

Rivera, Raquel Z. *New York Ricans from the Hip-Hop Zone*. New York: Palgrave Macmillan, 2003.

Ro, Ronin. *Gangsta: Merchandising the Rhymes of Violence*. New York: St. Martin's Press, 1996.

———. *Raising Hell: The Reign, Ruin, and Redemption of Run-D.M.C. and Jam Master Jay*. New York: Amistad, 2005.

Sarig, Roni. *Third Coast: Outkast, Timbaland, and How Hip-Hop Became a Southern Thing*. Cambridge, MA: Da Capo Press, 2007.

Shaw, William. *Westside: The Coast-to-Coast Explosion of Hip-Hop*. New York: First Cooper Square Press, 2002.

Simmons, Russell. *Life and Def: Sex, Drugs, Money + God*. New York: Three Rivers Press, 2001.

Smith, Wilfred Cantwell. *What Is Scripture? A Comparative Approach*. Minneapolis: Fortress, 1993.

Spencer, Jon Michael. *Blues and Evil*. Knoxville: University of Tennessee Press, 1993.

———. "The Blues as Black Therapy." *Black World*, November 1973, 28–40.

———. "Overview of American Pop Music in Theological Perspective," in *Theomusicology*, special issue, *Black Sacred Music: A Journal of Theomusicology* 8, no. 1 (Spring 1994): 209–10.

Stic.man. *The Art of Emceeing*. Atlanta: Boss Up, 2005.

Sylvan, Robin. *Traces of the Spirit: The Religious Dimensions of Popular Music*. New York: New York University Press, 2002.

Thiong'o, Ngugi wa. *Decolonising the Mind*. Portsmouth, NH: Heinemann, 1986.

Toop, David. *The Rap Attack: African Jive to New York Hip-Hop*. Boston: South End Press, 1984.

———. *Rap Attack 2: African Rap to Global Hip-Hop*. London: Serpent's Tail, 1994.

———. *Rap Attack 3: African Rap to Global Hip-Hop*. London: Serpent's Tail, 2000.

VIBE Books. *Hip-Hop Divas*. New York: Three Rivers Press, 2001.

Walker, Wyatt Tee. *Somebody's Calling My Name*. Valley Forge, PA: Judson, 1983.

West, Cornel. *Prophesy Deliverance! An Afro-American Revolutionary Christianity*. Philadelphia: Westminster Press, 1982.

Williams, Saul. *The Dead Emcee Scrolls: The Lost Teachings of Hip-Hop*. New York: MTV, 2006.

Wilson, William J. *The Declining Significance of Race*. Chicago: University of Chicago Press, 1980.

———. *The Ghetto Underclass: Social Science Perspectives*. Newbury Park, CA: Sage, 1993.

Woodson, Carter G. *The Miseducation of the Negro*. Trenton, NJ: Africa World Press, 1993.

Albums

Afrika Bambaataa and Soulsonic Force. *Looking for the Perfect Beat*. Tommy Boy TB-831, 1983, 33 ⅓ rpm, 12-inch.

Ambassador, The. *The Thesis*. Cross Movement CD-7711, 2005, compact disc.

Arrested Development. *3 Years, 5 Months, and 2 Days in the Life of*. Chrysalis CDP-21929, 1992, compact disc.

Blow, Kurtis. *Christmas Rappin'*. Mercury MDS-4009, 1979, 33 ⅓ rpm, 12-inch.

———. *Kurtis Blow*. Mercury SRM-1-3854, 1980, 33 ⅓ rpm, LP.

Bone Thugs~n~Harmony. *E 1999 Eternal*. Ruthless 88561-5539-2, 1995, compact disc.

Boogie Down Productions. *Criminal Minded*. B-Boy BB4787, 1987, 33 ⅓ rpm, LP.

———. *Ghetto Music: The Blueprint of Hip-Hop*. Jive 1187-1-J, 1989, 33 ⅓ rpm, LP.

Brown Sugar, music from the motion picture soundtrack. MCA 088 113 02802, 2002, compact disc.

Cee Lo Green. *Cee Lo Green . . . Is the Soul Machine*. Arista 82876 52111 2, 2004, compact disc.

Common. *Be*. GOOD/Geffen B0004670-02, 2005, compact disc.

———. *Finding Forever*. GOOD/Geffen B0009671-02, 2007, compact disc.

———. *One Day It'll All Make Sense*. Relativity 88561-1640-2, 1997, compact disc.

Common Sense. *Can I Borrow a Dollar?* Relativity 88561-1084-2, 1992, compact disc.

———. *Resurrection*. Relativity 88561-1208-2, 1994, compact disc.

DMX. *Flesh of My Flesh, Blood of My Blood*. Def Jam 314 538 640-2, 1998, compact disc.

———. *It's Dark and Hell Is Hot*. Def Jam 542 437-2, 1998, compact disc.

Dr. Dre. *The Chronic*. Death Row P2 57128, 1992, compact disc.

Fat Boys, The. *The Fat Boys*. Sutra SUS 1015, 1984, 33 ⅓ rpm, LP.

Geto Boys. *The Geto Boys*. Def American DEF 24306, 1990, 33 ⅓ rpm, LP.

Goodie Mob. *Soul Food*. LaFace 73008-26018-2, 1995, compact disc.

Grandmaster Flash and the Furious Five. *The Adventures of Grandmaster Flash on the Wheels of Steel*. Sugar Hill SH 557, 1981, 33⅓ rpm, 12-inch.

————. *The Message*. Sugar Hill SH 268, 1982, 33⅓ rpm, LP.

Hamilton, Anthony. *Ain't Nobody Worryin'*. So So Def 82876 74278 2, 2005, compact disc.

Hill, Lauryn. *The Miseducation of Lauryn Hill*. Ruffhouse/Columbia CK 69035, 1998, compact disc.

————. *MTV Unplugged 2.0*. Columbia, 2002.

Holiday, Billie. *The Best of Billie Holiday: The Millennium Collection*. Hip-O 314 589 995-2, 2002, compact disc.

Ice Cube. *Death Certificate*. Priority CDL 57155, 1991, compact disc.

Ice-T. *Rhyme Pays*. Sire/Warner Bros. 1-25602, 1987, 33⅓ rpm, LP.

Jay-Z. *Kingdom Come*. Roc-A-Fella B0008045-02, 2006, compact disc.

Jones, Mike. *Who Is Mike Jones?* Warner Bros. 49340-2, 2005, compact disc.

Kriss Kross. *Totally Krossed Out*. Ruffhouse/Columbia CK 48710, 1992, compact disc.

Kweli, Talib. *Eardrum*. Blacksmith/Warner Bros. 277244-2, 2007, compact disc.

Lil Jon and the East Side Boys. *The Kings of Crunk*. TVT TV-2370-2, 2002, compact disc.

Master P. *The Ghetto's Tryin to Kill Me!* No Limit NLR0188, 1994, compact disc.

MC Lyte. *Lyte as a Rock*. First Priority/Atlantic 0-96596, 1988, 33⅓ rpm, LP.

Mos Def. *Black on Both Sides*. Rawkus P2-50141, 1999, compact disc.

Nas. *Hip-Hop Is Dead*. Def Jam, 2006, compact disc.

Nelly. *Nellyville*. Universal 440 017 747-2, 2002, compact disc.

Notorious B.I.G., The. *Ready to Die*. Bad Boy 78612-73000-2, 1994, compact disc.

N.W.A. *Straight Outta Compton*. Ruthless SL 57102, 1988, 33⅓ rpm, LP.

Outkast. *Southernplayalisticadillacmuzik*. LaFace 73008-26010-2, 1994, compact disc.

Public Enemy. *Fear of a Black Planet*. Def Jam CK 45413, 1990, compact disc.

————. *It Takes a Nation of Millions to Hold Us Back*. Def Jam 527 358-1, 1988, 33⅓ rpm, LP.

Queen Latifah. *All Hail the Queen*. Tommy Boy TB 1022, 1989, 33⅓ rpm, LP.

Run-D.M.C. *Run-D.M.C.*, Profile/Arista PRO-1202, 1984, 33⅓ rpm, LP.

Salt-n-Pepa. *Hot, Cool, and Vicious*. Next Plateau PL-1007, 1986, 33⅓ rpm, LP.

Scott-Heron, Gil. *Small Talk at 125th and Lenox*. Flying Dutchman FDS 131, 1970, 33⅓ rpm, LP.

————. *Spirits*. TVT TVT 4310-2, 1994, compact disc.

Slim Thug. *Already Platinum*. Geffen B0003505-02, 2005, compact disc.

Smith, Will. *Greatest Hits*. Columbia CK 87076, 2002, compact disc.

T.I. *T.I. vs. T.I.P.* Atlantic 202171-2, 2007, compact disc.

2 Live Crew. *As Nasty as They Wanna Be*. Luke Skywalker CDXR 107, 1989, compact disc.

2Pac. *2Pacalypse Now*. Jive 41633-2, 1991, compact disc.

West, Kanye. *The College Dropout*. Roc-A-Fella B0002030-02, 2004, compact disc.

Young Buck. *Buck the World*. G-Unit/Interscope B0008030-01, 2007, compact disc.

Yo-Yo. *Make Way for the Motherlode*. East West/Atlantic 7567-91605-2, 1991, compact disc.

Films

The Art of 16 Bars. Directed by Peter Spirer. 2005. [United States]: QD3 Entertainment, 2005, DVD.

Beat Kings: The History of Hip-Hop. Directed by Mathematics. New York: Nature Sounds, 2006, DVD.

Beat Street. Directed by Stan Lathan. Orion Pictures, 1984. Santa Monica, CA: MGM Home Entertainment, 2003, DVD.

Brown Sugar. Directed by Rick Famuyiwa. Los Angeles: Fox Searchlight, 2002, DVD.

Freestyle: The Art of Rhyme. Directed by Kevin Fitzgerald. Organic Films, 2000, New York: Palm Pictures, 2004. DVD.

Hip-Hop: Beyond Beats and Rhymes. Directed by Byron Hurt. Media Education Foundation, 2006, DVD.

Jay-Z: Fade to Black. Directed by Patrick Paulson and Michael John Warren. Roc-A-Fella, 2004. Hollywood: Paramount Classics, 2005, DVD.

Krush Groove. Directed by Michael Schultz. Warner Bros. Pictures, 1985. Burbank, CA: Warner Home Video, 2003, DVD.

MTV Unplugged no. 2.0: Lauryn Hill. Directed by Joe De Maio. New York: Columbia Music Video, 2002, DVD.

Scratch. Directed by Doug Pray. Firewalk Films, 2001. New York: Palm Pictures, 2002, DVD.

Style Wars. Directed by Tony Silver and Henry Chalfant. 1983. Los Angeles: Public Art Films, 2004, DVD.

Wild Style. Directed by Charlie Ahearn. Wild Style Productions, 1983. Burbank, CA: Rhino Home Video, 2007, DVD.

index

Ralph Basui Watkins is associate professor of evangelism and church growth at Columbia Theological Seminary in Decatur, Georgia. Dr. Watkins blogs weekly at **www.hiphopredemption.org**, providing support for pastors, churches, professors, and students as they seek to engage the theology embedded in hip-hop culture. His website also features companion material—including discussion questions—for this book. You can also join the conversation on Dr. Watkins's Facebook page "hip-hop redemption" and check out his videos on Vimeo at www.vimeo.com/channels/218503.